THE DEANS OF DRINK

THE
DEANS
OF
DRINK

THE AMAZING LIVES & TURBULENT TIMES
OF HARRY JOHNSON & HARRY CRADDOCK
AS SEEN IN A NEW LIGHT

Being a narration of the Golden Eras of American & British cocktails as told through their careers & personal lives, with sundry historical notes & observations as well as cameos of others who made their mark, most notably Willy Schmidt, Ada Coleman, Paul Henkel Jr, James B Regan, Ruth Burgess, & William J Tarling; with rare photos & drawings; plus relevant walking tours of New York & London. Recipes included herein are not only of historic import, the reader will find form- ulas cre- ated by leading bartenders of today who are influenced by these masters.

Written by Anistatia Miller & Jared Brown

MIXELLANY LIMITED

Mixellany books may be purchased for educational, business, or sales promotional use. For information, please write to Mixellany Limited, 3 Eyford Cottages, Upper Slaughter, Cheltenham GL54 2JL United Kingdom or email jaredbrown1@mac.com

Photo credits: Museum of the City of New York pp 75, 76, 80, 82; Getty Images (UK) pp 137, 138; Savoy Group archives pp 141-143; all other images are from the authors' private collection.

First edition

ISBN 13: 978-1-907434-38-9
ISBN 13: 978-1-907434-39-6 (Limited edition)

British Library Cataloguing in Publication Data.
A catalogue record for this book is available from the British Library.

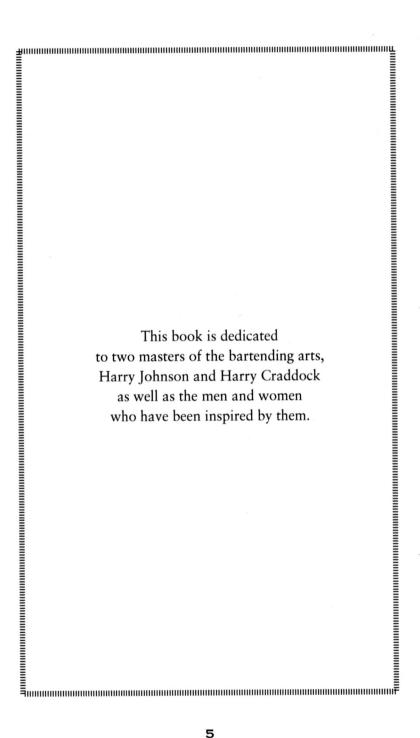

This book is dedicated
to two masters of the bartending arts,
Harry Johnson and Harry Craddock
as well as the men and women
who have been inspired by them.

CONTENTS

INTRODUCTION

What a moment it would have been. It could have been. Should have been. Harry Craddock, the passionate young bartender, sits down for a drink with Harry Johnson, the wizened industry veteran who wrote the book on cocktails and bar management. They were in New York at the same time, for a few years on and off in the early twentieth century. Craddock's star was rising, while the sun was settling into the dusk of Johnson's career as he became a "gentleman of leisure".

Johnson had so much advice to give. Craddock was eager to learn, and he was determined to hoist the cocktail pennant and fight for the profession. Just as Johnson tried to organize a bartenders' union, Craddock would go on to help found and serve as the first president of the United Kingdom Bartenders Guild. He would also write letters to the London newspapers, refuting anti-cocktail statements made by temperance advocates.

They start with a glass of champagne, a good vintage, perhaps a Pol Roger 1895, to prepare their palates for a round of Johnson's whiskey cocktails.

First, a toast to each other. Next, and with each following drink, a toast to the job. Such was the respect and commitment both had for bartending.

While Johnson's wisdom on management is unparalleled, Craddock quietly disagrees with him about the importance of buying spirits in bulk, maintaining good barrels in the cellar and understanding the fine points of barrel aging in-house. After all, this is the 20th century and bartenders have moved on from that. Johnson hopes aloud that the industry will someday find its way back to barrel aging.

At the time Craddock had been bartending in Chicago, bar boys in the better establishments were trained to cut perfect two-inch by two-inch cubes so that each drink would get identical dilution. For some drinks, they found nothing worked better than a large moulded or carved sphere of ice. (Yes, they were actually using ice balls in Chicago as early as 1899.) This, he knew, was where bartending around the world would go sooner or later.

Johnson smiles indulgently, and reminds Craddock that making drinks is only a small part of creating the guest experience. Craddock immediately agrees, but isn't swayed that easily off the subject of cocktails.

With the impertinence of youth, Craddock asks, "Exactly what is the difference between the Martine and the Martini?" Johnson replies, "One letter. One misplaced letter. That's all. You really should write a book one day, young Harry. Then they'll remember you in the years to come. In this industry, it's publish or perish."

"Then I will someday," replies Craddock, "But right now we have empty glasses and I've got a new drink I'd like you to try."

If such a meeting ever took place, it happened without single gin-soaked journalist in the room. Those members of the fourth estate flocked to these men, and to other great bartenders as well. They loved nothing more than to get in a few great drinks with these guys themselves. Then, to make a living from it, they wrote the stories of the bars. They captured for posterity the moments, the drinks, the culture of the bars as best they could at a ratio of three parts prose to one part vermouth.

Yet even posterity wakes up one morning having forgotten where it was just a century ago. So we had to dig. Join us now for a happy hour or two as we delve into the discoveries we made not just about these two Harrys, but about the world in which they moved and some of the other great bartenders who moved through it with them.

"Here's How!"

PART ONE

HARRY JOHNSON

CHAPTER ONE

FROM BIERGARTENS TO BARS

They came to American shores before the Pilgrims first sighted the spot that was to become known as Plymouth Rock. German emigration to North America commenced with the arrival of Dr Johannes Fleischer who, in 1607, accompanied the first English settlers who colonialized Jamestown, Virginia. This was the beginning.

Prompted by religious or political oppression and lured by the hope of land or business ownership, German migrants settled primarily in New York and Pennsylvania before the 1776 Revolution, introducing to the American cultural fabric the Christmas tree tradition, kindergarten education for children, hot dogs, hamburgers, and lager beer. The Eagle Brewery, opened in 1823 by German brewer David Gottlob Jüngling (later anglicized to Yuengling), was one of the first transplanted brewers to produce this longer-lasting, lighter style that overtook British-style ale consumption within a mere couple of decades.

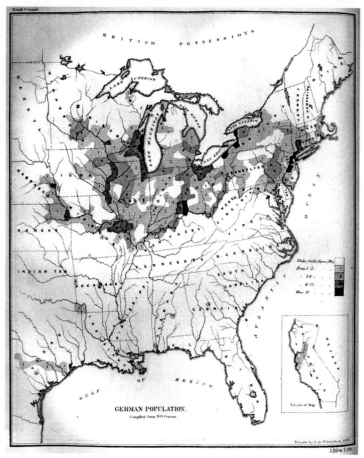

German immigration. (SOURCE: From The Statistics of the Population of the United States, Compiled from the Original Returns of the Ninth Census, 1872. Perry-Castañeda Library Map Collection.)

A concept imported from southern Germany, the *biergarten* (beer garden) accompanied these new arrivals as well. Unlike the Irish bars that proliferated before and immediately after the Revolution, beer gardens were family oriented. Lager drinking was only one of the attractions.

Minstrel shows and other theatrical acts, food and music were also on offer.

The most famous in those early days was Castle Garden, which opened in Castle Clinton at Battery Park on the southern tip of Manhattan. Originally constructed as the West Battery fortification to defend the city from British invasion during the War of 1812, the building was renamed Castle Clinton (after New York City Mayor Dewitt Clinton), in 1815, when it became the home of the Third Military District. In 1821, the US Army decommissioned the structure and leased it to the city as an entertainment facility.

1824: Theater performance inside Castle Garden (now: Castle Clinton National Monument), a former fort, in New York City.

Three years later, on 3 July 1824, Castle Garden opened on a rather grand scale, comprised of a theatre, resort, promenade, and beer garden. For a $5[1] admission,

---

1   Equivalent to $133.69 in today's currency.

ticket holders could stroll the riverside promenade, sipping the Mint Juleps and punch that were offered free of charge. Ice-cold, frothy lager refreshed diners in the immense beer garden. The theatre hosted Swedish operatic soprano Jenny Lind's first American performance, managed by PT Barnum. European dancing sensation Lola Montez performed her notorious and frenzied tarantella ("tarantula" dance).

Inventor Samuel Morse demonstrated his telegraph to the public at Castle Garden. Samuel Colt debuted his submarine there and the first steam-driven fire engine was also unveiled there before increasing waves of immigration into New York harbour forced the conversion of Castle Garden into an immigrant processing centre, in 1855, headed by the New York State Commissioners of Emigration.

The opulent beer garden legacy lives on in one famous name: Madison Square Garden was designed by Stamford White complete with a rooftop beer garden that towered high about the surrounding buildings and originally located at 26th and Madison Avenue in Manhattan. Opened in 1910, the Bohemian Hall & Beer Garden, situated across the river in Astoria, Queens, is the New York City's oldest, surviving beer garden that still remains in operation today.

Not all beer gardens were as plush as Castle Garden or Madison Square Garden. Smaller beer parlours nestled in the German neighbourhood bordered by Union Square and Tompkins Square, for example, offered beer garden seating in rear courtyards and on building rooftops where families could savour the cool air and lager on sweltering summer evenings. Lienau's, Brubacher's Wine Garden, and the Alhambra Gardens were all nestled in this neighbourhood. But the most famous was funded by piano magnate

William Steinway, who gave 26-year-old Hanover immigrant August Guido Lüchow a $1500[2] loan to purchase a café near Steinway's concert hall and piano showroom. (Lüchow had worked as a waiter and bartender at this establishment, owned by Baron von Melbach.) When he opened Lüchow's it quickly became the local haunt for a full complement of European music greats from Ignaz Paderewski and Antonín Dvořák, later for Oscar Hammerstein.

Postcard showing interior of Luchow's restaurant after 1902. Garden as seen from the café. Representation of daylight through skylights. Done before these same light fixtures were converted to electric by adding four additional goose-neck-mounted lights to each fixture.

Everyone who was anyone packed the establishment each night. From Diamond Jim Brady who had a room named after him and eating companion Lillian Russell to illustrator James Montgomery Flagg whose quote—"Through the doors

2   Equivalent to $38,565.57 in today's currency.

of Lüchow's pass all the famous people of the world"—was emblazoned at the entry to the main reception room. With its continued popularity, the beer garden was encased, in 1902, under frosted and etched stained glass skylights.

"From the Old to the New World" shows German emigrants boarding a steamer in Hamburg, Germany, to come to America. published in Harper's Weekly, (New York) November 7, 1874.

Aside from celebrities and business brokers, who else patronized and popularized this style of hospitality? The over six million German immigrants who arrived in America between 1820 and 1913. The largest influx landed after the Revolutions of 1848 forced numerous businessmen, professionals, politicians, and intellectuals to leave the German states. As they settled not only in the eastern seaboard but west beyond the Mississippi, a significant portion of these new arrivals opened saloons or worked in beer halls, pubs, and bars.

Between 1860 and 1900, the number of bartenders and saloon owners west of the Mississippi rose from under 4,000 to nearly 50,000. Forty percent were recent immigrants, and 25 percent of those were of German descent. Thirty percent of saloon proprietors in Colorado were German.

As America entered its Golden Age of Cocktails, a handful of German bartenders helped to shape the profession, introducing a new family of drinks into the cocktail repertoire and inspiring future generations with their attention to detail, service, and creativity. Some of these barmen had learnt their profession in Germany and brought with them well-deserved pride. Such was the case with "The Only William"—William Schmidt.

William Schmidt

CHAPTER TWO

THE ONLY WILLIAM

Born in Hamburg, Germany, Willy Schmidt gained fame there as a bartender, later stating that it was not entirely true that the best bartenders are Americans, or that the best fancy drinks are of American origin. He was quick to point out that he mastered his craft in Hamburg. Schmidt noted, in 1904, that:

> The finest mixed drinks and their ingredients are of foreign origin. Are not all of the superior cordials of foreign make? Is the pousse café a Yankee invention? No; and even the vaunted mint julep was concocted in Persia... Many of the best American drinks may be called revivals, rather than inventions.

With his small face and giant mustache, Schmidt arrived, in 1869, moving to Chicago. He took charge of opening team at the Tivoli Garden, in May 1873, with sixteen bartenders working under him and pulling in $12,000[3] in receipts within twelve hours. He was renowned for his acrobatic

---

3   Equivalent to $229,189.65 in today's currency.

bartending feats: throwing flaming and non-flaming drinks in graceful arcs. He was even better known for his ability to create drinks that would even convert people who swore they liked nothing stronger than lemonade.

Willy Schmidt, as captured by a newspaper illustrator, throwing a cocktail using two glasses to blend the mixture.

Schmidt moved to New York in 1884, where he tended bar at the Bridge Saloon. This may have been its name or simply a geographic moniker, as it was at the Manhattan end of the Brooklyn Bridge and was pulled down a few years later to make way for bridge approaches.

After twenty years of presiding over bars in the US, Schmidt took his first holiday and returned to Hamburg, in 1889, to visit his elderly parents (aged 90 and 92; they passed away the following year). Upon his return to New York, he took on a business partner and opened a place on Broadway near Park Row. When his partner died shortly after, the bar was sold. He stayed on as bartender, through several years and different owners. Eventually the bar was moved to 58 Dey Street, one door west of Greenwich Street, a site that is precisely at the heart of Ground Zero today. (The buildings on that part of Dey Street were torn down to make way for the World Trade Centre.)

William was renowned for creating new drinks. And at one point he was estimated to have invented a new one every day. He even created a "$5 cocktail"—proclaimed the costliest drink ever made—at a time when drink prices hovered around 15 cents[4].

> The foundation of the drink is made by crushing three or four sprigs of mint[5] and three lumps of sugar in a dash of water. This produces a blue tincture of mint. To this is added two ponies of the best brandy.
>
> The foundation is thus laid and the superstructure is now added. It consists of a pint of the finest champagne. Over this is placed a floor made of cracked ice, which supports the chief feature of the julep.
>
> A circular fence is next built about the top of the glass with slices of pineapple, banana, citron and orange and a few red roses.

---

4   Equivalent to $3.78 in today's currency. (Liquor taxes were much lower in those days.)

5   "You decry bruising the mint. Pray, sir, consider that for an old-time, genuine, soul-inspiring mint julep, the fresh fragrant mint is allowed to stand in the whiskey for at least an hour. Some prefer it to infuse for two hours. What are we to do when a julep is demanded at a moment's notice? Why, what can we do but gently bruise the mint, thereby achieving almost the same result instantly. Pray do not shoot those who gently bruise the mint."–William Schmidt, 27 July 1899

This vivid enclosure is then filled up with vanilla ice-cream.

Schmidt displays his $5 Cocktail, complete with its elaborate garnish.

A few choice berries of a bright colour are set on top of the white cream and some perfect sprigs of mint are made to tower above this miniature flower garden. When completed the julep, William declares, is the king of all mixed drinks and is to a bar what a beautiful flower is to a lady's boudoir. It suggests the fragrance and pure beauty of nature. To use his own expression, "It is the perfection of moist joy."

He was credited with an encyclopaedic knowledge of the classics, but he preferred talking with his customers, then inventing new drinks on the spot to suit their tastes and moods.

He authored two books: *Fancy Drinks and Popular Beverages* published by Dick & Fitzgerald (who also published Jerry Thomas' book), in 1891, and a much larger volume, *The Flowing Bowl*, published by Charles L Webster & Company the following year. Two books from different publishers in such a short time? Not exactly. *Fancy Drinks and Popular Beverages* simply contains the mixed drink chapters from *The Flowing Bowl*.

Despite packing hundreds and hundreds of recipes into his book(s), many of his drinks never made it into his tomes. These were often created when a journalist, writing about drinks asked him for a classic and, without telling the writer, he created them on the spot. Drinks like the Svengali Cocktail and The Angelus Cocktail made it into print as a result.

Svengali

1 part French Brandy
1 part absinthe
1 part French vermouth
2 dashes gomme syrup
Combine all ingredients in a glass with cracked ice.
Stir and serve.

The Angelus

30 ml Old Tom gin
2 dashes orange bitters
2 dashes curaçao
1 dash gomme syrup
1 dash absinthe

1 dash Italian vermouth
Combine all ingredients in an ice-filled mixing glass.
Throw or stir. For "an appetizing" variation substi-
tute absinthe for the Old Tom gin.

Schmidt retired in October 1904 rather than submit to the wage cut proposed by the bar's new owners as well as the introduction of barmaids to the establishment. Why the owner would have pressed such an acclaimed barman out of the business might be answered in the fact that his obituary, one year later, listed his cause of death in the State Hospital on Ward's Island as senile dementia.

Another answer might be found in the changing attitudes of the time. As William once said:

> A man in my profession should never forget he is a gentleman. However well he may mix a drink, much of the flavour is lost unless he serves it with politeness. But politeness has been dying out with the coming in of the quick lunch and the quick drink. They want speed, not quality, these days. And how can a true artist put soul into his productions if no time is allowed to him?

His obituary described the experience of sitting at his bar, clearly written by a man who had been there many times:

> To watch the 'Only William' at work was an education, and to hear his commentaries on the drink in the process of formation was to excite the appetite beyond all words. His drinks were creations. In his nimble fingers and his fervid heart there dwelt the genius of one of the earth's eccentric benefactors.
> And then the next day. Where again is such a man who can be the sponsor of such a day-after feeling

that William by his deftness guaranteed? Where are the 'Broadway Zephyrs,' 'Ambrosia Ambrosialized,' the 'Pleasant Surprise'? They are no more, for the 'Only William' is dead, and all Park Row mourns."

Willy Schmidt had German contemporaries and successors: George Kappeler, Henry C Ramos, Frank Meier, Eddie Woelke, Hugo R Ensslin are only a handful of names that precede and follow the name that eclipsed them all—Harry Johnson.

Harry Johnson

CHAPTER THREE

THE DEAN

We learn as time passes that age plays tricks with the memory. It's something that may haunt you as you read about Harry Johnson. It haunted us we as wrote this. But as we read and re-read the three major sources in which he narrated the story of his life, we realised that with each telling, the world had radically changed around him. Prohibition in America stripped him of his pride in his chosen profession. Fears and prejudice that stemmed from the First World War and grew in the period between then and the Second World War robbed him of in his ethnicity. His personal life was punctuated by multiple estrangements. You begin to realise why Harry altered portions of his story as the years passed. It wasn't just dottiness. He lived in a world that no longer appreciated or accepted what he had accomplished during his life, or where he had been born.

Let's start at the proverbial beginning.

Harry Johnson "was born aboard a German ship of which his father was the captain", on 28 August 1845, in Königsberg harbour in German-held Prussia (now known as Kaliningrad, Russia). At one time, he claimed that his father was an American citizen, but didn't mention his name.

When he was 75 years old, Johnson stated that in 1862, "he shipped aboard a vessel sailing between Hamburg and San Francisco. During the latter part of the voyage, he fell and broke his arm and hip and on the arrival of vessel in San Francisco he was placed in a hospital." The ship returned to Hamburg, leaving Harry to fend for himself with no friends or money. He claimed that the only job he was able to secure was at Smith's Hotel, cleaning vegetables and working his way up to manager within seven years. "After leaving San Francisco, he conducted hotels and restaurants in Chicago, Boston, New York, and Philadelphia," he concluded.

The Union Hotel was an example of a new style establishment for San Francisco in its early days, offering guests and walk-ins a high class of drink and liquor offering than found in conventional saloons.

There is no listing for a Smith's Hotel in the 1861 *San Francisco Business Directory*. However, there is one for the Union Hotel, which he mentioned in a 1910 interview: "It was away back in 1860 in San Francisco when I was only 15 years old that I began to mix drinks in the Union Hotel in that city." Situated at the corner of Merchant and Kearny Streets opposite Kearny Plaza, Madame Touchard operated the bar at the Union Hotel which offered a cocktail bar and billiard room to patrons.

Think about it. Prohibition went into effect 16 January 1920. He made this statement in April of that year to a US Department of State special agent. Harry covered up the fact that he was a bartender, a publican, a man who sold drink when he first arrived in the US and continued to earn his living doing so until the turn of the century so he could to America.

In his 1896 passport application he claimed to have arrived on 1 November 1853 and lived in California from 1853 until 1867 in California. Was it possible that Johnson arrived in San Francisco from Hamburg more than once? And only in 1862 did he find himself stuck with no way to return home.

However, the most mysterious and controversial point about Johnson's career is found in that same 1910 interview, in which he stated that:

> The drinks I invented and the way I mixed them attracted many patrons to the bar and I had so many requests from other bartenders to tell how I made this or that drink that I wrote a little book which I called the 'Bartenders Manual' and within six weeks my publishers had sold 10,000 copies at a price higher than I get for my new books which are very much larger."

What about this *Bartenders' Manual*?

There has been some speculation by fellow cocktail geeks Dave Wondrich and Mauro Majoub that the 1869

book *Haney's Steward & Barkeeper's Manual* published
by the Jesse Haney Company, which contained a few bartending tips was actually penned by the young Johnson.
But the other curiosity surrounding this first book is that
when he mentions it in the preface to his 1900 edition of
the *Bartenders' Manual* he tells another story:

> There was published by me, in San Francisco,
> the first Bartender's Manual ever issued in the United
> States. This publication was a virtual necessity—the
> result of a constant demand for such a treatise by those
> everywhere engaged in the hotel, bar and restaurant
> business. As a proof, ten thousand (10,000) copies of
> the work were sold at a price much larger than the
> present cost within the brief period of six weeks.

However the publication of his recipes came about,
word got around about Harry.

Johnson moved to Chicago, in 1868, to open a bar
that he said was "generally recognised to be the largest and
finest establishment of the kind in this country." It wasn't
long after that the 23-year-old Harry was contacted to take
part in a national bartending competition. Harry noted
that his invitation came because of his book when he said:
"Well, the book got scattered all over the country and the
newspapers wrote many stories about the book and me and
a very curious thing happened."

Giving a detailed account of this, the world's first bartending competition, Johnson recounted during the 1910
interview:

It was in 1869 that a man named Le Boeuf, who kept the finest bar room in New Orleans, wrote and asked me if I would enter a national competition in drink mixing. I went to New Orleans and there were competitors from St Louis, Cincinnati, Boston, New York and some other cities. The committee to judge us were partly people in the trade—hotel keepers and the like—but there were patrons of the bar too, who were judges and lawyers and merchants. The conditions were that each contestant in turn was to go behind the bar, arrange the working bench, as we call it, to suit himself, and when the contestant was ready a dozen customers were to step up and order each his favourite mixed drink.

Then it was Harry's turn:

When it came my turn a certain Judge Wilson led up a party of a dozen men and instead of giving me orders for cocktails, flips, juleps or whatever said the Judge: 'Well Master Harry, you can just mix us a dozen whiskey cocktails, and we'll see what you do with an order like that.'

WHISKEY COCKTAIL.
3/4 glass of fine shaved ice
2 dashes of gum syrup
2 dashes Boker's bitters
2 dashes curaçao
1 wine glass of whiskey
Stir up well with a spoon and strain it into a cocktail glass, putting in a cherry or a medium-sized
olive, and squeeze a piece of lemon peel on top, and
serve. This drink is without doubt one of the most
popular American drinks in existence.

Note that Harry used two mixing glasses held close together as shown here in a captionless illustration from his book that clearly immortalizes his competition-winning moment. Also, his juleps, on each side are finished with strainers in them.

I put a dozen water glasses on the bar in two rows of six each. On top of each row I made pyramids of cocktail glasses, three at the bottom then two and one at the top. Then I mixed what would make just a dozen cocktails, poured all of them into one large glass, covered that over the mouth of a similar glass, and using no strainer whatever, I held the two big glasses mouth to mouth and just opened a little bit of a crevice to let the cocktails pour out and keep the ice in.

Your drinks are ready gentlemen, I says, and honestly they gave me a cheer. After that it was 12 mint juleps, a favourite drink in New Orleans in those days."

MINT JULEP

(Use a large fancy bar glass.)
1 small table-spoonful of sugar;
½ wine-glass of water or selters;
3 or 4 sprigs of fresh mint; dissolve with sugar and water, until the flavour of the mint is well extracted; then take out the mint, and add ½ wine-glass of brandy (Martell).
Fill the glass with fine-shaved ice; stir well, then take some sprigs of mint, and insert them in the ice with stem downward, so that the leaves will be on surface in the shape of a bouquet; ornament with berries, pine-apple, and orange on top in a tasty manner; dash with a little Jamaica rum, and sprinkle with a little sugar on top; serve with a straw.
This drink is known not only in this country, but in all parts of the world, by name and reputation (see illustration, plate No. 8).

As you can imagine, Harry won the prize: $1,000[6] in gold plus a solid silver tumbler and mixing spoon.

---

6   Equivalent to $16,711.75 in today's currency.

PLATE No. 8.

CHAMPAGNE COBBLER.   MINT JULEP.

This elaborate garnishing technique was regarded a standard presentation practice at the dawn of the Gilded Age.

He went back to Chicago and enjoyed a run of extremely good luck until the Great Fire of 1871 put an end to his establishment and to his great fortune. As he recalled in the preface to his book, "But the conflagration of 1871 caused me a loss of $100,000[7] and, financially ruined, I was compelled to start life anew. It was at this time that I was taught the value of true friendship, for numerous acquaintances tendered me material assistance, which was, however, gratefully declined." A bookseller gave him $1,700[8], for a revised edition of his *Bartenders' Manual*, which aided in his financial recovery. Was this the 1871 *Bartender's Ready Reference* that was anonymously written?

However, a far more personal encounter would soon change his fate once again. He was about to meet Bertha.

---

7   Equivalent to $188,301.35 in today's currency.
8   Equivalent to $32,011.23 in today's currency.

CHAPTER FOUR

BERTHA

Born in March 1852, Bertha Paul emigrated from Germany on the ship *Cimbria*, arriving on 2 March 1871 in New York. She moved to Chicago by 1873, where she met Harry. They were married that same year on 2 October.

Johnson became a naturalised American citizen on 28 October 1875. According to his chapter entitled "Why Bartenders Should Have Their Own Union for Protection and Association" in the 1888 edition of his book, he returned to New Orleans that year hoping to unionise the profession "in an effort to procure for them sufficient wages, to give them a good, decent living, proper hours of labour, and for their general elevation as members of society. The effort at that time resulted unfortunately for the reason, principally, that the old, skilled bartenders, who retained the same situation for years, had passed away—men who supported well themselves, their families, and their clubs—and, in their stead, was a younger element in this avocation who, not knowing their work thoroughly, were careless and indifferent, and unable, drifted about from one place to another. The consequence was that they never became members of the club, and would not have been of benefit, had they done so. Under such circumstances, it was impossible to organise a beneficial society."

America celebrated its 100th anniversary the following year with the opening of the first World's Fair to be held in the United States. From 10 May through 10 November, the International Exhibition of Arts, Manufactures and Products of the Soil and Mine paid homage to the progress made in the century since the Declaration of Independence was signed in that city.

Harry secured a post as head barman at the recently opened Grand Exposition Hotel, supervising a staff of 2,000 employees. Situated at Girard and Lancaster Avenues, this "Saratoga of Philadelphia" was billed as the "largest hotel in the world", sporting 1,325 rooms that could accommodate 3,000 guests. The dining halls seated 1,500 guests. There was even a ball room that featured a live band every evening. It wasn't the only accommodation built on such a grand scale to accommodate the estimated 10 million people who came to the city for the celebrations.

Harry's sister Martha came to visit the couple and met Paul Henkel, a music teacher who had also emigrated from Prussia. They married in Philadelphia, in 1877, and lived at 235 South 12th Street. The couple relocated with their year-old daughter Clara to 242 North Tenth Street around the time their son, Paul Henkel Jr was born on 5 June 1880.

Young Paul played a pivotal role in Harry's life, and the restaurant industry, which we will discuss later.

DELMONICO'S

The Johnsons didn't settle in Philadelphia after the centennial celebrations died down. The couple moved, in 1878, to 32 Delancey Street in New York, with Harry registered in the 1880 US Federal Census as a "liquor salesman" and Bertha as "keeping house". He found a position at Delmonico's in New York, earning $100[9] per week as manager of both the bar and the wine cellar.

Opened in 1827 at 23 South William Street in lower Manhattan, Delmonico's began its life as a rented pastry shop before it moved, in 1837, to a lavish building at 2 South William Street (now 56 Beaver Street). Legendarily birthplace of such famed dishes as Delmonico steak, Lobster Newburg, Baked Alaska, and Manhattan Clam Chowder, it was there that Harry hosted Ulysses S Grant, who was so infamous for his love of compound libations that one news headline from around that time read "Grant Lingers Around Long Branch, Bartenders Weary of Making Fancy Drinks". Harry also served Russian Grand Duke Alexei Alexandrovich a Sherry Flip. He recounted years later that his bar receipts averaged $600 per day.[10]

A favourite haunt of Diamond Jim Brady and his eating companion Lillian Russell, Delmonico's afforded Johnson close contact with numerous captains of industry. Harry purportedly served Boss Tweed shortly after his arrival. He recalled: "Tweed was a daily customer there then. He would come in every afternoon with Harry Burnett, who was Tweed's contractor for paving Broadway from Battery to 14th street.

---

9   Equivalent to $2,305.07 in today's currency.
10   Equivalent to $13,830.41 in today's currency.

They both drank champagne, nothing but champagne except that if they dined there they would come out to me at the bar after dinner for a pony of brandy. That was brandy that Lorenz Delmonico told me he paid $100[11] gallon for. Those I served it to in ponies paid $1[12] a pony for it."

Delmonico's as it appears today in its lower Manhattan location.

There is a small problem with this story.

Boss Tweed had been in prison since 1876 and died in the Ludlow Street jail on 12 April 1878. It's more than

---

11   Equivalent to $2,305.07 in today's currency.
12   Equivalent to $23.05 in today's currency.

likely Harry served Harry Burnett who related stories about Boss Tweed.

One story we know is true.

WILLIAM R GRACE

Harry met William Russell Grace at Delmonico's. The city's first Irish-American Catholic mayor, Grace not only opposed Tammany Hall and Boss Tweed, he also aided in the break-up of the infamous New York City syndicate that operated the Louisiana State Lottery Company.[13]

The company had acquired a 25-year charter to conduct organised gambling in exchange for handing the State of Louisiana $40,000[14] per year from the proceeds. Inevitably, the operation became corrupt, swindling both those who purchased tickets and the state that was supposed to benefit.

During his second term in the mayoral seat, from 1885 to 1886, Grace accepted the Statue of Liberty as a gift from France on behalf of New York City and the United States. Aside from his political interests during those years, he was the founder of WR Grace and Company, a chemical conglomerate that he founded in 1854, after leaving Ireland during the potato famine and emigrating to Peru with his father and family, where he established a thriving business in guano, which was used in gunpowder and fertiliser man-ufacture. The company expanded into machinery and other industrial chemicals.

---

13   Not connected in any way with the current lottery corporation in the State of Louisiana.

14   Equivalent to $954,956.86 in today's currency.

Harry's reputation garnered interest from all corners, not just the world of municipal politics.

Published in both German and English, the 1882 edition of Johnson's book was a best-seller in its day.

The International News Company asked Johnson, in 1881, to revise and enlarge his bartenders' manual, printing 50,000 copies the following year, which the publisher paid him for in advance. This 1882 edition of Johnson's *Bartenders' Manual* contained 15 pages of bar management advice as well as 157 mixed drink and cocktail recipes.

LITTLE JUMBO

The Grand Street elevated station was a major destination for businessmen and politicians heading downtown to City Hall and Wall Street as well as shoppers who flocked to the department stores along Grand Street itself.

"With that money and what I had saved while with Delmonico I started the Little Jumbo on the Bowery [119 Bowery] near Grand Street, next to Coogan Brothers," Johnson fondly remembered. "It was a little bit of a place, only fourteen feet wide, but I put a lot of money into its fixtures and furniture, and my friends said I was crazy to go to the Bowery and open the most expensively furnished bar in New York." He obtained a five-year lease on the property from John Callahan for a cost of $2,500[15].

---

15   Equivalent to $55,705.82 in today's currency.

Historian Alvin Fay Harlow later positioned Harry's place on the top shelf of what sort of establishments existed on the Bowery:

> Some of these were respectable places—as respectable as a saloon can be. Other genteel resorts were the Café Loesling, already mentioned, and Harry Johnson's Little Jumbo at 119 Bowery; Johnson, the inventor of piquant, ambrosial drinks whose formulae were all in his Bartender's Manual, magician whose liquid rainbow in air from shaker to glass enthralled the beholder, and who could mix a drink for five persons so that it filled five glasses to the brim without a drop left over. Beside his door a famous signboard more than four feet high listed some one hundred of his mixed drinks in pyramidal form, beginning at the top with the Gin Fizz and so proceeding downward, gradually flaring through names of increasing length such as Egg Nogg, Alabazam, Shandygaff, Tom Collins, Brain Duster, Happy Moment, Hannibal Hamlin, Sitting Bull Fizz, and New Orleans Punch to the base of the cone.

Topping this obelisk "was a small gold elephant, from which the place took its name—Jumbo, being the famous elephant in the London Zoo, a favourite of Queen Victoria's which was later acquired and exploited with great profit by Phineas T Barnum."

Harry's former Delmonico's customers brought their friends, attracting stockbrokers, politicians, bankers, all the masters of industry who worked in and around the Financial District and City Hall. Harry worked long hours to make his new bar succeed, mixing his own creations whilst his staff served up straight spirit drinks.

GIN FIZZ
RAINBOW
EGG NOGG
ALABAZAM
GIN RICKEY
ROYAL FIZZ
MINT JULEP
SHANDYGAFF
TOM & JERRY
TOM COLLINS
POUSSE CAFE
BRAIN-DUSTER
CLARET PUNCH
WHISKEY SOUR
BRANDY TODDY
HAPPY MOMENT
WHISKEY SLING
PORT SANGAREE
CATAWBA PUNCH
SHERRY COBBLER
ABSINTHE FRAPPE
HANNIBAL HAMLIN
SITTING-BULL FIZZ
MANHATTAN COOLER
NEW ORLEANS PUNCH
MANHATTAN COCKTAIL

A recreation of the Little Jumbo sign board as it appeared in Henry Collins Brown's 1927 book In the Golden Nineties.

WHITNEY & HIS SOCIETY

But the Bowery was a neighbourhood in flux even then. It was the territory of The Bowery Boys, who had battled with the infamous Five Points gang, The Dead Rabbits, since the 1860s, the Bowery was lined with missions, flop houses, all manner of saloons, brothels, and cheap clothing shops. The Third Avenue elevated train loomed overhead, darkening the sidewalks. The saving grace was that Harry was situated close to the Grand Street Station, where Wall Street and City Hall workers boarded the train along with shoppers heading home from the large department stores along Grand Street itself. This provided him with good daytime and weekday business.

To ensure that his place maintained a certain level of clientele on the weekends, Harry relieved his night barman at 7 AM on Saturday and worked through until 4 AM Monday morning. From 1 AM until 4 AM on Saturday, he stood outside: Not to encourage more customers but to turn away anyone who looked "rough" or drunk or under age. He personally kicked out any who caused trouble. He took pride in only selling top-shelf spirits. He later commented, "I was told that I couldn't follow those rules on the Bowery, but I did."

Temperance advocates pushed to enforce the state Excise Law that banned liquor sales on Sundays. Harry had his own encounter as he recalled:

> There was a man named [David J] Whitney who was a famous crusader against excise offenders. He with several friends came to Little Jumbo one Sunday. I was warned and could have kept them out, but I did not. Whitney ordered a soft drink, but some of his friends

ordered whiskey. Then I stepped up to Mr Whitney
and said: 'It may be offensive to your friend to drink
whiskey. If so, tell them not to do it. They don't need
to do that to prove that I am violating the excise law.
I admit it.

Whitney asked Harry to call on him at his office the
very next day. "I did and he talked to me like a Dutch uncle,"
Harry remembered. "I thought he was going to indict me,
but the whole of his talk was telling me to preach to other
publicans to keep orderly places, such as mine."

Although David Whitney and the Society for the Prevention of Crime—of which he was the president—were
forthright and true dealing in their endeavours, there were
people who attempted to exploit its altruistic cause for their
own advantage.

George Herbener, proprietor of Stein's Hotel at The
Bowery and Fifth Street, lodged a complaint, in April 1884,
with the police about George Wright, who claimed that he
was an agent for the Society for the Prevention of Crime.
The affidavit alleged that on Sunday, 30 March 1884,
"Wright entered Herbener's saloon and said he was one of
Mr Whitney's officers and that he had caught him violating the Excise Law. Mr Herbener then alleges that Wright
hinted that the trouble could e easily fixed. The complainant
[Herbener] then introduced ex-Judge John A Dinkel to the
defendants as Mr Hess and stated that the latter was his
partner. Mr Wright then informed Mr Dinkel that he had
seen men playing cards and drinking beer and again hinted
that it would be worthwhile to keep the matter from the
society. The saloon keeper went to Captain McCullogh [of
the Fifth Street police station] and made him acquainted

with the above story. The Captain advised the man to mark a $10[16] bill and place it in an envelope and give it to Wright. Captain Mcullogh detailed detectives Bissert and Robinson to arrest the man who took the envelope."

On 2 April 1884, "Harry Johnson, a saloon keeper at No 119 Bowery, and Wright entered the saloon. The saloon keeper handed the envelope to the agent for the society. He was taken into custody by the detectives, who arrested Wright, but the envelope could not be found on his person. Ex-Judge Dinkel, however, found it in the gutter near the place where Wright was arrested... Harry Johnson, the saloon keeper, who went to the place with Wright says that the latter entered the saloon and that he had a strong case of violation of the Excise Law against a man, and that he expected the matter would be fixed for a half century [meaning for $50[17]]."

"'You take the money,' Johnson says Wright said to him, 'and I'll make it all right with you. You know it wouldn't do for me to compromise a case, as it might break me.'"

In the end it did.

Three days later, Wright appeared before Justice Gormanat the Essex Market Police Court, accusing Captain McCullogh and Herbener of conspiring to defeat the purpose of the Society for the Prevention of Crime. Herbener also charged that "Wright had represented that he worked under Charles Rillings, the superintendent of the society, who was to get $40[18] of the $50 demanded, while Wright would retain the balance.

---

16   Equivalent to $234.55 in today's currency.
17   Equivalent to $1,172.75 in today's currency.
18   Equivalent to $234.55 in today's currency.

Wright further denied that he was an agent of the society and explained "that six weeks ago Charles Rillings, a friend of his, had called on him at a bookbindery where he was employed and engaged him to sell fire escapes for Mr DJ Whitney...Wright said he did not prosper in the new business, and after a while Rillings said to him: 'I am an officer of Mr Whitney's society. If you see any violations of the Excise Law, report the same to me and I will take action.'"

Wright had found twenty men playings cards and drinking beer and that beer was sold to him on the Saturday night and the same situation occurred on the Sunday night.

According to Wright, Herbener handed him an envelope to square the complaint, Wright testified that he threw the envleope behind the bar in disgust and was then arrested.

Whitney, who was present in court, remarked that neither Wright nor Billings had any connection with the Society for the Prevention of Crime.

Billings had been discharged two months earlier, continuing that: "I believe there are four or five men banded together to use the name of the society for their own advantage. They have before, as in this case, made complaints to the Excise Board when they have no right to do so."

THE EXCISE

Harry's friend Mayor Grace sided with German bar owners, when he was re-elected in 1885, and sought to amend the Excise Law "so as to permit the sale of ale and beer on Sunday, except between the hours of 10 AM and 4 PM." (Hotel bars, restaurants, and private clubs had already figured out how to dodge the law by exclusively serving drinks in their guest-only spaces and private dining rooms.)

Tammany Hall member Abram Stevens Hewitt was elected New York City mayor, in 1886, and staunchly campaigned against the city's vice and red light districts, particularly the Bowery. During his term, a ban on the sales of beer and liquor on Sundays was introduced. But with every saloon boasting a busy side or back door the law was impossible to enforce.

Captain, Inspector and Chief of the New York Police, George W Walling wrote in his memoirs about the difficulties faced by police on the beat:

> Let the police do what they may in the matter of making arrests for violations of the excise law, they cannot stop them. Suppose, in the first place, a policeman, in citizen's clothes, enters a saloon on Sunday and sees beer and spirits sold freely. He arrests the bar-tender, who is taken before a magistrate. The law says that if the accused demands a trial by jury it must be granted him, the amount of bail being fixed at $100[19]. Then the case goes to the General Sessions, where it is placed on file, never to come up again probably while he lives. Why? Because I suppose there are not far from twenty thousand such cases on file there now, and the machinery of the court of General Sessions is totally inadequate to deal with them."

Why were Sundays such a target?

---

19   Equivalent to $ 2,430.80 in today's currency.

Most men worked a six-day week, and Sunday was the only full day left for drinking at saloons. Thus, proprietors made their best money on the Lord's Day.

Yet Harry wasn't too fussed about the growing political pressure that surrounded his profession and his bar. He had other things on his mind.

Like most business owners in those days, Harry lived above his business. When his mother Amalia Johnson died at 73 years of age after a long illness, on 1 December 1884, the funeral service took place in Harry's apartment above Little Jumbo.

When not crafting creations or managing the bar, Johnson conducted a school, instructing the valets of wealthy gentlemen how to stock a private bar and to make mixed drinks. This made the news almost as much as his Little Jumbo did.

A New York correspondent for the *Pioneer Press* reported, in 1885, that

> The newest affectation in this line is the private bartender. He is not an importation from England, but wholly, so far as I can learn, a New York production... The idea is said to have been original with Alfredo Talharin, a rich young Brazilian, who had known only the harsh and primitive distillations of his native land before coming to New York to spend the winter.

Knowing that he would soon return to his home in Buenos Aires, Talharin put his valet "under the instruction of Harry Johnson, noted among New York able drinkers as a mixer of complicated beverages." Word got around town amongst the city's dandies. And the correspondent noted that "already a dozen valets of distinguished dudes have become proficient, and their masters' rooms are provided with cabinets from which the newest cocktails and the queerest mixed drinks are turned out."

This Illustration shows how to keep your working bench in condition. Copyrighted, 1888.

An illustration of Johnson's preferred bar design as seen in the 1888 edition of his book.

It seems that early in 1881 Harry took a 3½-year lease on a store and basement owned by Peter Wassung at 14 Stanton Street, which the New York Clipper reported as being a pool-room. But in Phillips Business Directory of New York City for 1881 and 1882, Wassung's name is the only one associated with this address. Was this possibly the location of Johnson's bartending school?

Johnson was also busy working on the expanded and illustrated edition of his *Bartenders' Manual*. "I have only been back from Europe a couple of weeks and am busy getting out a new edition of my barkeeper's manual," he enthusiastically commented to a reporter. "This will be the seventh edition I have published in eighteen years and will be illustrated. It will contain a good many new mixed drinks, including several hot ones."

Printed in both English and German by the International News Company, Johnson's 1888 edition was lavishly illustrated with images of Harry demonstrating his Whiskey Cocktail pyramid, the perfect bar design, and the first illustrations of a Martini Cocktail and other drinks as they were presented in the day. His bartending tips now extended to 29 pages and the recipe section was expanded to include 186 formulas, including the earliest documentation for the Manhattan Cocktail, Martini Cocktail, and Vermouth Cocktail.

MARTINE COCKTAIL.

Spelled correctly on the recipe, the Martini Cocktail was mislabelled here.

MARTINI COCKTAIL.

(Use a large bar glass.)

Fill the glass up with ice;

2 or 3 dashes of gum syrup (be careful in not using too much);

2 or 3 dashes of bitters (Boker's genuine only);

1 dash of curaçao or absinthe, if required;

½ wine-glass of old Tom gin;

½ wine-glass of vermouth.

Stir up well with a spoon; strain it into a fancy cocktail glass; put in a cherry or a medium-sized olive, if required; and squeeze a piece of lemon peel on top, and serve (see illustration, plate No. 13).

MANHATTAN COCKTAIL.

(Use a large bar glass.)

Fill the glass up with ice;

1 or 2 dashes of gum syrup, very carefully;

1 or 2 dashes of bitters (orange bitters);

1 dash of curaçao or absinthe, if required;

½ wine-glass of whiskey;

½ wine-glass of vermouth;

Stir up well; strain into a fancy cocktail glass; squeeze a piece of lemon peel on top, and serve; leave it for the customer to decide, whether to use absinthe or not. This drink is very popular at the present day. It is the bartender's duty to ask the customer, whether he desires his drink dry or sweet.

VERMOUTH COCKTAIL.

(Use a large bar glass.)

¾ glass of shaved ice;

4 or 5 dashes of gum;

2 or 3 dashes of bitters (Boker's genuine only);

1 wine glass of vermouth;

2 dashes of maraschino;

Stir up well with a spoon; strain it into a cocktail
glass, twist a piece of lemon peel on top, and put a
cherry in if required, and serve.

Like many great bartenders, Harry concealed his private
life. Perhaps the biggest and best-kept secret was his son and
daughter with Bertha. Meet Herbert and Sigrid Johnson.

Johnson's name is clearly visible on the signs to the left and right of the staircase.

CHAPTER FIVE

HERBERT & SIGRID

An article appearing in the 29 July 1895 edition of New York's *The World*, titled "Side Doors: Open All Over the City to Those in the Secret and with Money" sets the scene for next phase in Harry's life. That year, the city's drinks trade pried open a loophole in the Sunday Excise Law: "One wet hour closed the dry day. When last midnight came saloons all over town that had been deserted through the day threw open their doors, and white-coated bartenders served the thirsty who had long waited for something cool and refresh them."

"In front of many saloons a long line had formed. Many men who naturally would have been in bed long before waited for that single hour, from Sunday midnight to 1 AM Monday, which is not covered by the law, and when it is legal to sell anything that a man wants to buy. Along Park Row, the Bowery, Third Avenue, Houston Street, in the Tenderloin and uptown saloons had an extraordinary business."

Harry was no longer on the Bowery.

After he returned his lease back to John Callahan, around November 1889, he opened a new place in a much better area, a few blocks away from Delmonico's in the Wall Street district. He opened Johnson's Café & Restaurant in the basement of William R Grace's office building at One and Two Hanover Square. There he served lunch and drinks. Naturally, Mr Grace was a daily customer.

(Ironically, the restaurant that has occupied that space since 1972 is called Harry's Cafe & Steak, opened by Harry Poulakakos, who is not a blood relation, but had also worked at Delmonico's for over a decade before launching his own restaurant, now owned and operated by his son Peter.)

Again, Harry's personal life triggered another career transition. He handed day-to-day operations over to his staff, in 1896, remembering later he "went to Europe again, thinking I'd never go into the business anymore." There was more to this statement than Johnson ever admitted in the press.

On 7 February 1896, his son Herbert was born. Four months later, Bertha took their baby to Germany and never officially returned to live with Harry. Johnson applied for a US Passport on 16 June 1896, stating he would return to New York in one year. It was time to pay attention to his family, his wife, his child, to the life he never talked about in the press.

TRAINOR'S PLACE

One cold December day after his return, in 1897, Harry walked up Broadway and stopped for a drink at Trainor's Hotel & Restaurant at 33rd Street. He knew the owner from his Little Jumbo days.

Squat and rotund, with sandy hair and moustache, James Trainor had a reputation for running a respectable establishment during daylight hours, and employing local "toughs" to tend bar at night. This plan had two flaws: occasionally a respectable customer would wander in at the wrong time. If that customer ran afoul of the staff, they would throw him out—hard—and it would make the newspapers. Also, the toughs began lining their pockets with Trainor's revenues.

So, when Trainor spotted Harry in the bar, he told him that he wanted to sell the place. He encouraged Harry to look at his books, which disclosed that Trainor lost $27,000[20] due to staff embezzlement. Trainor went to the barber shop for a shave. When he returned, Harry wrote him a deposit for $50,000[21] and took possession of a five-year lease on the place. Trainor had second thoughts and tried to buy his way out of the sale the next day, adding another $10,000[22] to sweeten the deal. Harry turned him down.

Johnson put an additional $40,000[23] into redoing the façade and interior, selling off the old windows and woodwork, but kept Trainor's name on the door. To keep close track of the business, he took up residence in the hotel.

Opened in 1873 by James Trainor, the establishment was one of the city's best known cafés and hotels. According to a 1909 article in *The New York Times*:

> It was Trainor's place that gave the name 'Tenderloin' to the section of the city where dandies went to trip the life fantastic. It is said that Inspector Williams, coming to the Tenderloin as Captain of the West 30th Street Station ate his first meal as precinct commander

---

20   Equivalent to $ 736,681.01 in today's currency.
21   Equivalent to $ 7,366,810.10 in today's currency.
22   Equivalent to $ 272,844.82 in today's currency.
23   Equivalent to $ 1,091,379.30 in today's currency.

at Trainor's. The next day he went back to Mulberry Street on business, and to some of his associates is said to have remarked: 'I am through with chuck steak; it is tenderloin for me where I am now,' and since that day the district has been best known as 'The Tenderloin.'

The Raines Law was passed, on 23 March 1896, in the New York State Legislature. Amongst its many provisions, it prohibited the sale of alcohol on Sunday except in hotels. The state considered any establishment to be a hotel if it had ten rooms for lodging and served at the very least sandwiches with its liquor.

Thus, under new ownership, Harry's old Little Jumbo became known as the Little Jumbo Hotel (or Rapid Transit Hotel). Dozens of saloons added small furnished bedrooms and applied for hotel licences. Harry was very fortunate to have acquired a legitimate, landmark hotel.

Harry appeared in the news once again, slightly exaggerated as was normal in the days of "yellow journalism". A notice in the 2 December 1897 edition of *The World* announced that "Trainor's Hotel [at 1289-1291 Broadway] was sold yesterday by James J Trainor to Harry Johnson, who formerly conducted a resort on the Bowery, and the latter took immediate possession" for a reported price of $120,000[24].

The 1888 *Illustrated New York: The Metropolis of To-Day* best describes the wisdom in Harry's decision to purchase: "The results have borne out Mr Trainor's sound judgment, for this quiet strictly respectable house is fully patronized by the best classes of the travelling and city public,

---

24   Equivalent to $ 2,728,448.20 in today's currency.

who truly appreciate economical accommodations of this kind in the business centre of the city. A large restaurant 100 feet in depth is attached and very handsomely fitted up, and where meals are served at moderate prices. The catering is liberal and the cooking first-class, and the majority of the guests dine here, in addition to a heavy outside patronage. The bar (distinct from dining room) is splendidly fitted up, and is fully stocked with purest and best of wines and liquors. It should be recollected that Trainor's Hotel is so central that elevated railroad trains and street cars to all parts of the city can be taken from its door."

Trainor's is the dark building on the right, with one storey peeking above the level of the passing elevated trains.

Sensibly priced for midtown Manhattan, Trainor's Hotel offered gentlemen (no female guests) the choice of fifty well-appointed rooms for $1[25] per night, $5[26] per week, in a great business location situated near the theatre district.

An item in *The New York Times* on 26 April 1898 referred to the establishment as Johnson's Hotel. Another article from that same year noted that Harry Johnson of Trainor's Hotel bailed out Sergeant "Buck" Taylor, a former member of Theodore Roosevelt's Rough Riders who had been arrested and unjustly accused of defrauding another hotel keeper. (Taylor's friends rallied and paid off his outstanding bill at Morrison's Hotel for him, then pleaded with the management to drop the charges.)

Harry didn't stay for the full term of the lease. A message from Heidelberg, Germany arrived. His daughter, Sigrid, was born on 2 March. He sailed in June to meet her and visit with the rest of his absent family.

On his return, Johnson sold the hotel, in April 1899, for precisely what he paid to Trainor plus the cost of the refurbishment to Louis Schmidt. Rather than explaining to the press about his growing family in Germany, he claimed that he had been ill for several months and planned a trip to Europe, noting that "rather than be bothered running the place from across the Atlantic he decided to sell it."

He applied for a passport for both himself and Bertha in October of that year, hoping she and the children would return with him. Sadly they didn't. But he still had hope.

---

25   Equivalent to $ 27.28 in today's currency.
26   Equivalent to $ 136.42 in today's currency.

HIS MAGNUM OPUS

Erected in 1900, The Endymion at 352 West 117th Street was situated half a block away from New York's verdant Morningside Park and Columbia University's campus. It was the sort of place where the residents picnicked in the park on Sundays, listening to the brass band and savouring the fresh air that was part of the good life in uptown Manhattan. The apartment building itself featured six- and seven-room, *en suite* apartments fitted with hot water, steam, and windows that faced the outside. "Hall service" and an elevator made this accommodation more posh than the standard Manhattan living space. The building even supplied the residents with ice from an on-premise ice machine.

This was his way of showing Bertha that he would focus on his family life, not the bar or hotel business. He even installed a live-in maid—a 17-year-old German servant named Rose Schacht. Bertha was also listed as a member of the household on the 1900 Federal census, even though she still lived in Germany with their children Herbert and Sigrid.

Settled in to a new environment, Harry completed a second revision of his manual, the final culmination of everything he ever knew about bartending and bar management, expanding the front section from 29 to 135 pages of advice on operations and training.

The vermouth cocktail category exploded well beyond the Martini, Manhattan, and Vermouth Cocktails within a mere twelve years. Once again, Harry was the first to fully document the growth of the vermouth cocktail category among the 256 recipes. This book featured twenty concoctions that display the versatility of both dry and sweet vermouth mixed with different spirits.

This edition also marks the first appearance in print of the Marguerite, the esteemed predecessor of the Dry Martini and another Martini Cocktail variation, the Bradford[27] a la Martini. And it portrays the drying of the American palate with the call for Plymouth Dry Gin instead of Old Tom or Hollands styles in the documentation of the Bijou Cocktail, Olivette Cocktail, Turf Cocktail, and Marguerite Cocktail.

BIJOU COCKTAIL.

(Use a large bar glass.)
¾ glass filled with fine shaved ice;
1/3 wine glass chartreuse (green);
1/3 wine glass vermouth (Italian);
1/3 wine glass of Plymouth gin;
1 dash of orange bitters.
Mix well with a spoon, strain into a cocktail glass;
add a cherry or medium-size olive, squeeze a piece
of lemon peel on top and serve.

BLACK THORN.

(Use a large bar glass.)
3 or 4 dashes of absinthe;
3 or 4 dashes of bitters (Boker's genuine only);
½ wine glass of French vermouth;
½ wine glass of Irish whiskey;
Stir up well with a spoon, strain into a medium
sized wine glass and serve.

---

27   For decades after this, bartenders referred to a shaken Martini as a Bradford.

BRADFORD A LA MARTINI.
(Use a large bar glass.)
¾ glass of fine-shaved ice;
3 or 4 dashes of orange bitters;
The peel of one lemon into mixing glass;
½ wine glass of Tom gin;
½ wine glass of vermouth;
Shake well with a shaker, strain into a cocktail glass,
put a medium-sized olive into it and serve.

BRAZIL COCKTAIL.
(Use a large bar glass.)
¾ glass of fine-shaved ice;
3 or 4 dashes of bitters (Boker's genuine only);
3 or 4 dashes of absinthe;
½ wine glass of French vermouth;
½ wine glass of sherry wine;
Stir up well with a spoon, strain into a cocktail
glass, putting in a cherry, squeeze a piece of lemon
peel on top and serve.

IMPERIAL COCKTAIL.
(Use a large bar glass.)
¾ glass full of fine-shaved ice;
1 or 2 dashes of orange bitters;
1 or 2 dashes of absinthe;
½ wine glass of French vermouth;
½ wine glass of maraschino;
Stir up well with a spoon, strain into a cocktail
glass, putting in a cherry, squeeze a piece of lemon
peel on top and serve.

KLONDYKE COCKTAIL.
(Use a large bar glass.)
¾ glass full of fine-shaved ice;
3 or 4 dashes of bitters (Boker's genuine only);
½ wine glass of applejack;

½ wine glass of French vermouth;
Stir up well with a spoon, strain into a cocktail
glass, putting in a medium-size olive, squeeze a piece
of lemon peel on top and serve.

LITTLE EGYPT.

(Use a large bar glass.)
¾ glass full of fine-shaved ice;
2 or 3 dashes of bitters (Boker's genuine only);
2 or 3 dashes of absinthe;
2 or 3 dashes of vermouth;
1 wine glass of sherry;
Stir up well with a spoon, strain into a medium size
wine glass and serve.

MARGUERITE COCKTAIL.

(Use a large bar glass.)
Fill glass ¾ full of fine-shaved ice;
2 or 3 dashes of orange bitters;
2 or 3 dashes of anisette;
½ wine glass of French vermouth;
½ wine glass of Plymouth gin;
Stir up well with a spoon, strain into a cocktail
glass, putting in a cherry, squeeze a piece of lemon
peel on top and serve.

MONTANA COCKTAIL.

(Use a large bar glass.)
¾ glass full of fine-shaved ice;
2 or 3 dashes of anisette;
2 or 3 dashes of bitters (Boker's genuine only);
½ wine glass of French vermouth;
½ wine glass of Sloe gin;
Stir up well with a spoon, strain into a cocktail
glass; squeeze a piece of lemon peel on top and
serve.

MORNING COCKTAIL.
(Use a large bar glass.)
Fill up a glass with finely shaved ice;
2 dashes of curaçoa;
2 dashes of maraschino;
2 dashes of absinthe;
3 or 4 dashes of bitters (Boker's genuine only);
½ wine glass of brandy;
½ wine glass of vermouth;
Stir up well with a spoon; strain into a cocktail
glass, putting in a cherry; twist a piece of lemon peel
on top, and serve.

OLIVETTE COCKTAIL.
(Use a large bar glass.)
¾ glass of fine-shaved ice;
1 or 2 dashes of gum;
3 or 4 dashes of orange bitters;
3 or 4 dashes of absinthe;
1 wine glass of Plymouth gin;
Stir up well with a spoon, strain into cocktail glass,
putting in an olive, squeeze a piece of lemon peel on
top and serve.

REFORM COCKTAIL.
(Use a large bar glass.)
¾ glass of fine-shaved ice;
2 or 3 dashes of bitters (Boker's genuine only);
½ wine glass of French vermouth;
½ wine glass of sherry;
Stir up well with a spoon, strain into a cocktail
glass, putting a cherry into it, squeeze a piece of
lemon peel on top and serve.

ST JOSEPH COCKTAIL.
(Use a large bar glass.)
¾ glass of fine-shaved ice;

1 or 2 dashes of gum syrup;
2 or 3 dashes of bitters (Boker's genuine only);
½ wine glass of French vermouth;
½ wine glass of Scotch whiskey;
Stir up well with a spoon, strain into a cocktail glass; putting a medium-size olive into it, squeeze a piece of lemon peel on top and serve.

SILVER COCKTAIL.

(Use a large bar glass.)
1 or 2 dashes of gum:
2 or 3 dashes of orange bitters;
3 dashes of maraschino;
½ wine glass of French vermouth;
½ wine glass of gin;
Stir up well with a spoon, strain into a cocktail glass; squeeze a piece of lemon peel on top and serve.

THORN COCKTAIL.

(Use a large size bar glass.)
Fill glass ¾ full of fine-shaved ice;
1 dash of orange bitters;
½ wine glass of calisaya;
¼ wine glass of old Tom gin;
¼ wine glass of French vermouth;
Stir well with a spoon, strain into a cocktail glass, putting in a cherry, squeeze a piece of lemon peel on top and serve.

TRILBY COCKTAIL.

(Use a large bar glass.)
Fill up with shaved ice;
2 dashes of absinthe;
2 or 3 dashes of orange bitters;
2 or 3 dashes of "Parfait d'Amour;"
½ wine glass of Scotch whiskey;

½ wine glass of Italian vermouth;
Stir up well with a spoon; strain into a cocktail
glass, putting in cherries, and squeeze a piece of
lemon peel on top, then serve.

TUXEDO COCKTAIL.

(Use a large bar glass.)
¾ glass full of fine-shaved ice;
1 or 2 dashes of maraschino;
1 dash of absinthe;
2 or 3 dashes of orange bitters;
½ wine glass of French vermouth;
½ wine glass Sir Burnett's Tom gin;
Stir up well with a spoon, strain into a cocktail
glass, putting in cherry, squeeze a piece of lemon
peel on top and serve.

TURF COCKTAIL.

(Use a large bar glass.)
¾ full of fine shaved ice;
2 or 3 dashes of orange bitters;
2 or 3 dashes of maraschino;
2 dashes of absinthe;
½ wine glass of French vermouth;
½ wine glass of Plymouth gin;
Stir up well with a spoon, strain into a cocktail
glass, putting in a medium size olive; and serve.

Printed in both New York and London, the book's
preface spelt out in no uncertain terms the intense pride
that Johnson had in his accomplishments as a bartender. He
narrated how he got into the profession, what he achieved,
and why he took it upon himself to create this timeless reference work. Even today, many bar owners and managers
agree that his instructions are as viable today as they were
over a century ago.

In conclusion to this final testament to the profession he was leaving behind he wrote:

> The principle I desire to instil is that this vocation—that of eating and drinking—to be properly successful, must be conducted by the same legitimate methods as any other monied enterprise that appeals directly to the public. It furnishes a necessity, just as does the clothier, hatter, and shoe-dealer, and, in itself, is an honourable means of livelihood. It should not be regarded by the proprietor or employee as a special means of securing the patronage of friends, as a possible avenue of good luck, or as a chance to gain by nefarious opportunities. It should be managed alone in an earnest, honourable manner. Believe in yourself, and others will have faith in you.

However, unbeknownst to Harry, his most audacious project and "swan song" to the hospitality profession was about to take shape.

CHAPTER SIX

PABST'S GRAND CIRCLE

Another German expat, former steamboat captain Frederick Pabst headed up the world's largest brewery, the Pabst Brewing Company, at the turn of the century. He marketed his lager from coast to coast, making his brand visible on more than just labels and advertisements. He did it by investing in real estate from coast to coast, border to border.

Over the course of twenty-five years, hundreds upon hundreds of Pabst taverns and beer gardens were created and leased all over the country. The establishments exclusively served the brewery's products and proudly displayed the company logo. Then he ventured beyond the obvious.

His rival, Joseph Schlitz, converted one of his Milwaukee beer gardens into Schlitz Park, a sprawling resort that featured a concert pavilion, a dance hall, a bowling alley, refreshment parlours, and live performers. Its centrepiece was a three-story pagoda-like structure atop a hill that offered a panoramic view of the city. Pabst was not to be outdone.

He opened Pabst Park. The eight-acre complex boasted a 15,000-foot-long roller coaster, a "Katzenjammer palace" fun house, and "the smallest real railroad in the world." Wild west shows were booked on a regular basis, and live orchestras performed daily through the summer.

Then he trumped this move with his entry into New York City, in 1899, opening the Pabst Hotel in the heart of Manhattan, at 42nd Street between Broadway and Seventh Avenue. Making another wise investment, Pabst went into partnership with an experienced bartender-turned-hotelier named James B Regan, who he signed on as its proprietor.

Who? Haven't heard of him?

JAMES B REGAN

As a shoeless boy on the oyster banks of New Jersey, he stood with his father gazing at Manhattan. His father said to him, "I give you all of that—to make good in."

He found a bar boy job in Old Earle's Hotel on Canal Street, squeezing lemons. He worked his way up the ranks from the Fort William Henry Hotel, the Grenoble, and the Buckingham before attaining a bartender post at the famed Hoffman House Hotel.

Being at one of the city's top watering holes helped build his reputation and his list of contacts. His customers ranged from the rich and famous to writers and sports people. So it's no surprise that when he decided to open his own place in fashionable Westchester county, he had investors lined up with cash to spare.

Situated near the Morris Park race track, The Wood-mansten Inn welcomed the cream of New York society from the Vanderbilts to the Astors. Regan proved that he was not only a great bar talent, he was a convivial hotelier.

Pabst, who had opened a brewery, in 1896, at 606 West 49th Street, was keen to get a foothold in Manhattan before his rivals. Regan was on his radar scope.

The Pabst Hotel stood on the spot where the New Year's Eve ball now descends each year at Times Square.

The beer baron and the hotel owner opened the Pabst Hotel on 11 November 1899 to great fanfare and a cost of $350,000[28].

The seven-storey hotel housed "thirty-five sleeping apartments, handsomely furnished, and twenty-one bath-

---

28   Equivalent to $ 9,549,570.00 in today's currency.

rooms, appointed with enamelled tubs, showers and marble washstands."

The 100-seat café on the Broadway street level was dressed in Louis XV style polished marble, carved wood, mirrors, and crystal. The dining room above was equally fitted out in Renaissance decor.

Extending out below the street, the 260-seat Rathskellar was decked out in grand German Empire drawing room fashion in rich woodworking and eye-pleasing murals. Naturally, the house served Pabst Blue Ribbon Beer.

At a time when a hotel might only have a couple of bathrooms on each floor, the Pabst Hotel was a glimpse of the luxurious future for guests.

The *New York Herald* reported: "There is not in all New York a more attractive place than the Rathskeller, which is nightly thronged by those who make the metropolis of the Western World one of the brightest of cities. In front and at the sides of the Pabst Hotel on opera nights is a long line of carriages. The broad and carpeted staircase is thronged by the men and women of fashion."

The Pabst Hotel only stayed open until 1902, when the tunnel work for the Independent Railway Train (IRT) drew a path right through the Rathskeller and electrical plant below, forcing its closure. Regan went back to his Woodmansten Inn on a full-time basis for a few years and Captain Pabst headed up Broadway, in 1900, opening the grandiose Pabst Harlem Restaurant & Music Hall at 243 West 125th Street.

This cavernous space was built more than a decade before the similarly shaped (and considerably larger) Grand Central Terminal opened in 1913.

Harry Johnson's nephew Paul Henkel Jr had been toiling as a reporter for publisher Craige Lippincott of Philadelphia's JB Lippincott & Company publishing house, which not only printed and distributed books but also the popular *Lippincott's Monthly Magazine*. Journalism was a very high-paid profession, especially at the entry level. So it was easy for Paul to be lured by his uncle Harry into the hospitality industry. When Pabst opened the Harlem establishment, 21-year-old Paul was hired on as an auditor and receiving clerk. Throughout his life he would state that his uncle Harry got him to change careers.

Still determined to maintain a hotel presence after the close of the Pabst Hotel, the beer baron identified another bartender-turned-hotelier with whom to collaborate—Harry Johnson himself.

The 19 May 1901 edition of *The New York Times* reported that the plans "for Pabst Grand Circle Hotel and Park Theatre were filed... by Architect John H Duncan" for an estimated build-out cost of $450,000[29].

Not wishing to take on such a huge project on his own, at the age of 55 Johnson went into partnership, on 27 February 1902, with Mathias Bock the affable, neatly-bearded, 38-year-old caterer at the Arion Club. (Located at 59th Street and Park Avenue, this German-oriented private club occasionally hosted dinners for up to 1,800 of its members.)

Although it was set to open in 1902, the Pabst Grand Circle was unveiled to the public on 12 January 1903 at Eighth Avenue and 58th Street. With an unimpeded view of Central Park, the complex consisted of the New Majestic Theatre, a café and dining room, roof garden, and a hotel.

---

29   Equivalent to $13,078,760.00 in today's currency.

The two lower floors are occupied by cafés and a dining room. The main dining room is on the second floor, and can be reached by elevators either from the Circle or the Fifty-eighth Street side. This large, brilliant room, decorated in white, French grey and gold, is of a Louis XIV treatment. The drapings of the many large windows and the wall coverings are of red velour. Hardwood floors are carpeted in red. There is a music gallery in the west hall. All the rooms are illuminated by bands of light on the columns and large gold sunbursts in the ceiling—a new effect. The general impression of this dining room is bright and roomy. In summer, tables will be set on the balconies, which project from the windows."

The men's cafe and bar and ladies' cafe on the first floor are treated in a modern adaptation of Louis XIV with mosaic floors, wax finished oak wainscoting, touched with gold, and richly carved and ornamented ceilings. The walls above a twelve-foot wainscoting are covered with red velvet, which makes an excellent background for the oil paintings which are hung about the room....The back bar is treated in a novel manner with polished brass brackets, to display to best advantage the beautiful glasses."

An art gallery on the café level contained paintings valued at $150,000[30], which were "the personal property of Harry Johnson." Paul Henkel Jr reminisced, in 1947, with a reporter: "Beer, of course, wasn't the only beverage sold: at the opening of the art gallery a thousand bottles of champagne were consumed, which led Paul Henkel, managing director of the emporium, to observe that here was 'an all-time high in art criticism.' Many of the paintings had

---

30   Equivalent to $ 3,856,560.00 in todays currency.

frames like keyholes, the better to dramatize their [intimate] character, which gives you an idea."

Thirty-six flambeau gas torches on the cornice gave the edifice an imposing façade. The Louis XIV Room on the second floor was fitted with more paintings, backgrounded by regal red velvet and finished oak wainscoting touched with gold. Huge gold sunbursts embellished the ceiling. Columns throughout the building were fashioned from Levant marble with bronze caps.

Standing at what is now Columbus Circle, at the southwest corner of Central Park, the Pabst Grand Circle was a jewel in the city's crown..

Food service included an à lá carte menu even in the evenings, a rarity at the time. An eight-piece orchestra entertained diners and imbibers, led by David Blimberg. The complex attracted the likes of Manhattan A-listers David Belasco, Flo Ziegfeld, George M Cohan, Lillian Russell, Marie Dressier, Marc Klaw, Lotta Faust, A. L, Erlanger, Victor Herbert, Emma Carus, Blanche Ring, J. P. Morgan and Colonel Jacob Ruppert, owner of the Yankees baseball team.

Johnson hired his nephew, 23-year-old Paul as managing director, the city's youngest person to hold the position. With an ear for music, Henkel hired a song-and-piano act billed as Berlin and Snyder to play in the café. Among the patrons to hear the duo was Lee Shubert who whisked Irving Berlin away to be a singer in the musical *Up and Down Broadway*. Ted Snyder became the publisher of Berlin's first big hit, "Alexander's Ragtime Band", and later became a partner in the music publishing firm, Waterson, Berlin, and Snyder.

THE WIZARD OF OZ

The inaugural production at the Pabst Grand Circle's theatre, The Majestic, was staged on 21 January 1903. It was the Broadway premier of L Frank Baum's musical adaptation of his best-selling book *The Wizard of Oz*. It was a proverbial overnight success. (The film version is still a favourite around the world.)

The 15 August 1903 performance made even bigger headlines in *The New York Times*. The famed tea merchant, yachtsman and socialite Sir Thomas Johnstone Lipton arrived not so quietly at the theatre with a group of yachting friends.

Onlookers gathered to shake hands or just to get a glimpse of the America's Cup's most famous loser.

1903: Bobby Gaylor and the chorus from the musical adaptation of Baum's The Wizard of Oz *when it opened at the Majestic Theatre.*

Three policemen escorted him safely to the door through the exuberant mob. But even the production company had all eyes on Sir Thomas, especially when actress Lotta Faust looked up from the stage at his box and sang the show's "popular 'Sammy' song" with a few twists in the lyrics:

> Tommy, Oh! Oh! Sir Tommy.
> You're a dandy, from your feet up.
> Tommy, when you come cruising, we're scared
>   of losing
> That blessed cup.

After several encores, Lotta added a new line in her final reprise:

Tommy, Oh! Oh! Sir Tommy.
When you come wooing, there's something doing,
Around my heart.

The audience's roars of approval were deafening after each verse. Then finally, Lipton "rose from his seat and tossed a large bunch of American Beauties [roses] on the stage."

THE END OF AN ERA

With this kind of cachet, you can well imagine that Johnson's venture did a heavy trade. But his involvement didn't last for long. He slipped and fell in the hotel just after it opened. His injuries were bad enough that he got a passport in March 1903 and went to Germany for treatment. He signed power of attorney to Paul.

Frederick Pabst died the following year on New Year's Day 1904. Then came a downturn in fortunes for the project.

The business had huge overhead: $20,000[31] per year for the lease on the land alone. Plus, profits from all beer sales went directly to Pabst. The company was unable to pay $3,207[32] for goods ordered between December 1903 and February 1904.

It was then discovered the Johnson suffered the same dilemma as John Trainor had back in 1897 with the staff of his Trainor's Hotel. The *New York Herald* reported that:

31   Equivalent to $ 514,207.54 in today's currency.
32   Equivalent to $ 82,453.18 in today's currency.

"Although the bar did a flourishing business, the restaurant, through bad management, has lost money steadily. Several of the waiters were convicted in the Court of Special Sessions of substituting smaller checks for those which the customers actually paid, and there were numerous thefts."

The corporation of Johnson & Bock was forced into bankruptcy. A notice appeared in *The New York Times* on 18 February 1904.

The Globe and Commercial Advertiser listed Mathias Bock's death, on March 4, weeks before his 41st birthday. By the time Johnson returned from abroad, his only job was to quit-claim on the lease and to sign over his half of the interest to Eugene Schliep to clear his portion of the company's $45,000[33] debts. In every report, the media pointed out that Johnson as the famous bartender and author. While his personal assets had been protected by the laws of incorporation, Harry laid low for a while.

He did not go abroad again until 1907. When he did, the 62-year-old hotelier's passport did not mention an occupation. On the trip after that, in 1909, he called himself "a gentleman of leisure". He did the same the following year, and spent time living in London, Paris, and Berlin, selling his bartenders' manual and teaching private barmen.

Tempered by fire, Paul Henkel Jr became manager of Keen's Chop House around the time it began allowing women in the restaurant. And he was responsible for expanding it (and at one point came up with the odd idea of keeping chickens on the roof to ensure fresh poultry).

Keen's may claim they have allowed women to dine there since 1905, but that didn't mean women could eat in

---

33   Equivalent to $ 1,156,967.00 in today's currency.

any room in the restaurant. In 1908, Henkel faced two law-suits, each demanding $10,000[34], from a pair of suffragettes he refused to serve in the main dining hall, which was for men only. Upon being refused service, one of the women launched herself onto a chair and gave an impassioned equal rights speech. It's said she had the support of the 200 men in the room until she began a "scathing denunciation" of men and of Henkel in particular. In his defence, he later pointed out the ladies had not been refused service at Keen's, just in that room.

Henkel owned a share in the Keen's Chop House chain, with outlets at the opulent Ansonia on the Upper West Side and two venues in midtown Manhattan. He was often referred to as Keen's owner.

This wasn't enough for Henkel who, in 1909, also opened the Kaiserhof Restaurant, a sprawling German *rathskeller* situated directly across the street from the old Metropolitan Opera House at the corner of Broadway and 39th Street.

Uncle Harry returned from a year-long trip to Germany, in 1910, to check on Paul's progress with the media out in full force to interview the legendary barman. Johnson had kept the apartment at The Endymion despite his long absences, and once again he took residence without Bertha and the children.

Certainly, Johnson was around to advise Henkel when he sold his share in the Keen's enterprise, in 1913, staying on as manager and took office as the president of the city's Society of Restaurateurs, which he had helped to found.

Harry's health was still not the best, so in October of that year he returned to Berlin.

---

34   Equivalent to $ 257,103.77 in today's currency.

Johnson as he appeared in his 1916 passport application photo.

CHAPTER SEVEN

WAR

War was declared on 28 June 1914—the Great War, the First World War—between Germany and the Ottoman Empire on the one side with France and the British Empire on the other. Although the US did not initially enter into the conflict, there was a rising anti-German sentiment among American citizens and politicians.

Johnson was living in the wrong place at the wrong time. That much was certain. He also faced another form of bias. "Hyphenated Americans" had become a common derogatory term in the States ever since President Wilson used it in 1889 to refer to immigrants who maintained allegiance to their home countries. Bertha had given Harry no choice but to divide himself between the old and new worlds. When he applied to return at the American Embassy in Berlin, in 1916, he raised a number of eyebrows with officials.

Required to complete an Affidavit to Overcome Presumption of Expatriation, Johnson stated: "I came abroad in 1913 purely for my health and this has been and is the only reason for my long stay. I have relatives in the United

States. At present I have no business or property interests in the States. I was formerly owner and manager of a hotel in New York City. My income is not sufficient for the Federal Income Tax."

On the actual passport application he provided proof that "Sigrid Johnson, holder of Department passport 558019 issued April 27th, 1915 is a daughter of [the] applicant and Herbert Johnson who applied for and received a Department passport through the Consulate at Mannheim is a son of [the] applicant."

Bertha was not mentioned. Sigrid's 1915 passport application explains why. Harry's health declined in October 1913 because Bertha filed for a divorce.

Sigrid Johnson as she appeared in her 1915 passport application photo.

Harry had every intention of living and working in Germany, to be near his family. But by the time he realised his business life had killed any hope of reigniting his personal life, it was too late.

When he gave a statement to a special agent at the US Department of State, in 1920, he said he went to Germany "to defend a lawsuit in connection with the settlement of family property in Munich. Before the case came up for trial, the lawyer whom he had engaged was drafted into the German Army. After delays caused by postponement and his illness, the case was settled in September 1916."

Who knows how much property and other assets had to be sorted out between the couple after forty years of marriage with Bertha living in Germany for nearly half of it?

When he finished with the painful climax of this portion of his life, he found himself in Rotterdam, waiting for the return ship to New York.

He had brought the draft of a hotel manual that he was working on, in 1913, along with the manuscript for the *Bartenders' Manual* that he intended on having translated and printed in French, German, and Dutch (at least one newspaper reported that he did print it in a number of foreign languages). He was then advised by the steamship officials that "if he considered his manuscript and books of any value and wished to use them after, he had better not taken them with him as the English officials [at the ship's first port of call, Liverpool] examined all books etc., and they might not be returned."

Johnson stored the books and papers with the Nederlaneche Handel Naatschat for safekeeping, paying them in advance by arrangement with his New York bank. He returned home to a different world.

Newspapers in New York and other cities published lists of German inhabitants' names and addresses who resided throughout the US, labelling them as "Enemy Aliens," effectively inviting neighbours to instigate hostile actions. US President Woodrow Wilson issued a proclamation, in November 1917, that restricted the employment and travels of German males over the age of 14 who were living in the United States. *The New York Times* reported that the order directly affected 130,000 men in the Greater New York and northern New Jersey regions.

Herbert Johnson as he appeared in his 1919 passport photograph.

This anti-German nativism and encroaching Prohibition convinced Harry to lay low, in 1917 and 1918, as America entered the war. Herbert worked in Bruschel, Baden through the last half of the war as a clerk at a cigar manufacturer, and then trained in a law firm with American connections. Moving to Copenhagen, Denmark, where he stayed until in 1919 when he received permission to move to the US as an American citizen from the Department of State, Herbert made his way to New York, where he told officials he was staying with Harry at The Endymion.

Johnson as he appeared in his 1921 passport photo.

He may or may not have for shared the apartment for very long. Harry headed back to Rotterdam to retrieve his manuscript and books, in 1920, despite the challenges of getting a US passport at a still sensitive time for German Americans. He returned in September 1921 to New York. Herbert also went to Germany that year, but returned to an apartment at 152 Lenox Road in Brooklyn. Two years later he had an apartment at 10 E 40th Street.

Sigrid found herself on Long Island as a governess to the three daughters of Loomis and Henrietta Taylor, who lived on Halsey Road in fashionable Southampton. (The trail grows cold on Sigrid after 1925, save for a possibility that she married, in 1928, a man named Herbert Purves.)

It was fairly apparent that Harry was closer with his nephew Paul than he ever was or ever would be to his own children as the years streamed by.

Johnson never stopped travelling and selling his books on bartending throughout Europe as Prohibition took hold in the America and the world spiralled toward an economic depression of monumental proportions.

Taking one of his last trips abroad and returning home in 25 July 1929, we find Harry living in a tidy brownstone on a tree-lined block that is even closer to Morningside Park than The Endymion. He moved to 362 West 121st Street. It was the perfect place to spend his final years, when he wasn't travelling to Germany, that is.

When we published *Spirituous Journey: A History of Drink, Book Two* in 2010, we thought we had uncovered Johnson's death: at the age of 89 on 26 February 1933, and buried in Green-Wood Cemetery in Brooklyn. We based that information on the fact that this man was the only Harry Johnson to pass away between 1927 and 1933 within the five New York City boroughs, The age match was perfect.

With no other facts available to confirm or refute this, we accepted it as the closest we could get to the truth. But we never stopped looking.

As we write this, vital records—passport applications and other US consulate documents dated after 1925—are still being digitized and archived in databases. One key document that completes our search was uploaded as we were doubling checking details in hindsight, after we went to press on 15 January 2013.

It appears Harry Johnson made a final voyage to Berlin late in 1929 either to visit or accompanied by a new wife, Martha Johnson. Residing at Bellealliancestrasse 65, Berlin SW 61, the couple might have chosen to spend the holidays there. On 5 January 1930 at 19:00, Harry Johnson died from "cardiac inefficiency and weakness due to old age." Martha was by his side with Dr E Ense in attendance. He was interred in Heilig kreuz-Friedhof in Berlin-Tempelhof.

His passport (the number matches the application with his photo and signature) was cancelled and returned to Martha. His naturalization certificate was returned to the US for cancellation by the State Department. We eagerly await the release of additional documents to discover more about his widow.

There were no flowing obituaries published at his passing in America as there were for Jerry Thomas and Willy Schmidt who preceded him to the grave. The city and the country were still struggling with Prohibition. Harry had outlived most of his customers, and he was a continent away. Sadly, his body did not carry him a couple years further to return home and witness Repeal: An act his nephew Paul Henkel Jr fought hard to bring about as president of the Society of New York Restaurateurs, even leading a delegation to Washington DC to meet with President Herbert Hoover in March of 1932. Johnson's legacy also lived on in other ways.

Charles E Graham & Company of Newark, New Jersey, republished Johnson's book in 1934, after Prohibition was repealed and America was mixing cocktails again. Was Paul responsible for reviving his uncle's memory? Chances are pretty good he instigated the media coverage that was seen during the 1930s.

One example was fairly extensive. Selmer Fougner, *The New York Sun* journalist who wrote the syndicated "Along the Wine Trail" column paid tribute over two articles, in April 1937, about Johnson's accomplishments (even though they were slighted exaggerated at points).

Paul never let people forget that his uncle Harry "invented the cocktail" until the day he died on 26 August 1957.

Harry's was a successful life, a tumultuous life, and at times a sad life. One thing he never did in his 84 years was give up or accept anything less than his dream. At a time when American politics and economic pressures changed how everyone in the world lived, he continued to find his way from bartender to bar owner to hotelier to advisor and mentor.

At the end of the day he was proud of what he had accomplished. As Harry said: "I am not boasting, but I'm glad of the chance to say that it takes training to be a publican and that a publican's chances for success are just in proportion to his observance of business rules. And the best of those rules are to keep an orderly place and sell good stuff. Oh, yes, it does not hurt if he knows how to mix drinks properly."

For this lesson alone, we are most grateful.

CHAPTER EIGHT

JOHNSON'S NEW YORK

Many of Harry Johnson's old haunts still exist in New York. And a visit to some of these key landmarks will give you an idea of how vibrant the city's drinking culture was back in those late Victorian days. Here is a route that will guide you from his first job in Manhattan to his final resting place in Brooklyn.

LOWER MANHATTAN

Delmonico's, 55 Beaver Street, New York: Upon his arrival in New York in 1878, Harry Johnson secured a job at the opulent Delmonico's. Managing both the bar and the wine cellar, Johnson served legendary figures including former US President Ulysses S Grant and Russian Grand Duke Alexei Alexandrovich. The restaurant still looks much as it must have when Harry worked there.

Harry Johnson's Café & Restaurant, One & Two Hanover Square, New York: With the newly enforced Sunday laws and declining condition of the Bowery Harry was convinced it was time to find another place to ply his craft. He opened a spacious café and restaurant in the basement of former New York mayor William Russell Grace's office building 1887. The next year, he published the third, largely expanded edition of his Bartenders' Manual. This time the book had illustrations! The workload wore him down by 1896. So, Harry handed over the establishment to his staff and headed to Germany to be with Bertha and his son Herbert who had moved there earlier in the year. It is easy to find. Look for the sign that says Harry's (the name is now coincidental, but what a coincidence that another Delmonico's waiter also named Harry, nearly a century later, invested his life's savings into opening a restaurant on the same spot; it is now run by his son).

Little Jumbo, 119 Bowery, New York: Carefully saving his $100 per week Delmonico's salary plus the advance payment on the publication of 50,000 copies of his Bartenders' Manual, in 1881, Johnson leased a 14-foot wide store front at this location. The bar name was Little Jumbo. He decked out his venue with high quality fixtures and furnishings that were uncommon in the area. His friends told him he was crazy to open such an expensively fitted bar in the Bowery, but he did.

32 Delancey Street, New York: The Johnsons moved to this address in 1878 when Harry got his job at Delmonico's.

MIDTOWN MANHATTAN

Trainor's Hotel & Restaurant, 33rd St & Broadway, New York: When he returned to New York in the winter of 1897, Harry took a five-year lease on Trainor's Hotel & Restaurant on Horace Greeley Square from owner James Trainor for around $100,000. (He also lived in this hotel without Bertha or his son.) With clientele such as officers of Teddy Roosevelt's Rough Riders and an array of Tenderloin district dandies, Harry operated a thriving business for two years before deciding to sell the place to Louis Schmidt in 1899 after he returned from meeting his new-born daughter Sigrid on a visit to Germany.

Keen's Chop House, 72 West 36 Street, New York: Henkel was often referred to an the sole owner of Keen's, although in truth, he was only a partner. During his time with Keen's, he also helped found the city's Society of Restaurateurs in 1912 and headed it for decades. During Prohibition he was an active lobbyist for repeal, which offered him the opportunity to lead a delegation to Washington and meet with President Hoover. The bar inside this landmark eatery is one of the best preserved examples of what Johnson thought was the perfect "work station" for mixing drinks.

Kaiserhof Restaurant, 39th and Broadway, New York: An injury just after opening the Grand Circle Hotel forced Johnson to travel to Germany for treatment. He left Henkel to bear the burden of managing operations and paying the complex's huge overhead. By the time he returned in 1904, he and his partner were forced to file for corporate bankruptcy of their joint venture and he signed over his interest in the hotel. Henkel became manager of both Keen's Old English Chop House and the sprawling Kaiserhof Restaurant, which was located across the street from the Metropolitan Opera House. Uncle Harry kept a watchful eye on his nephew as Henkel opened Keen's branches at the Ansonia on the Upper West Side and two additional midtown venues.

Pabst Grand Circle Hotel & New Majestic Theatre, Columbus Circle, New York: With a build-out cost of $450,000[35], the Pabst Brewing Company opened its second Manhattan hotel and restaurant complex, the Pabst Grand Circle, in collaboration with Johnson and partner Mathias Bock. Unveiling the massive and opulent project nearly a year later than originally scheduled, the complex consisted of a café and dining room, roof garden, hotel, art gallery (which presented Johnson's personal art collection, worth about $4 million in today's currency), and the New Majestic Theatre. Johnson hired his nephew, 23-year-old Paul Henkel Jr, as the complex's managing director. The theatre's first production was the Broadway premier of the musical *The Wizard of Oz*.

UPTOWN MANHATTAN

The Endymion, 352 West 117th Street, New York: Completed in 1900, The Endymion offered tenants spacious six- and seven-room apartments with all of the modern conveniences: en suite facilities, hot water, steam heat, and

---

35   Equivalent to $11,569,670.00 in today's currency.

windows that faced the outside. Tenants also enjoyed elevator service, "hall service", and an ice machine in the building. Situated steps away from Morningside Park, Johnson also hired a live-in servant named Rosie to further entice Bertha to return to America with their children. Johnson maintained this address until the late 1920s.

362 West 121st Street, New York: Johnson moved this single-family brownstone town house during the late 1920s. In his late eighties the move to a larger residence is surprising, but its proximity to Morningside Park was also very appealing.

CHAPTER NINE

LIQUID TRIBUTES TO HARRY JOHNSON

How far and for how long has Harry Johnson's influence exerted itself on the bartending profession? We searched around the globe, asking seasoned veterans and rising young stars to show what they learned by studying Johnson's style of drink creation. Which of his now-classic drinks inspired a new creation for a new generation?

MAURO MAJOUB
MUNICH, GERMANY

My recipe is inspired by the Manhattan Cocktail in Harry Johnson's 1888 edition. Curiosity Rover is a machine used to explore Mars. Launched in 2011 it landed on Mars the following year. Its mission: survey the Martian climate and help future human exploration. The barman is much like the Curiosity Rover, always trying new explorations and new dimensions. And my cocktail is as red as Mars.

Cocktail Curiosity (2011 Mars)
4 cl rye whiskey
2 cl Aperol
1 cl Italian sweet vermouth
1 dash absinthe (optional)
1 dash Fernet Branca
1 teaspoon raspberry marmalade
Shake over ice and strain into a chilled cocktail
glass.

My other favourite cocktail from the same book is the Martini Cocktail. First of all because it is the first time the Martini was documented in print and because the Martini is very similar to the Negroni—almost the same family of drinks.

TAKUMI WATANABE
NARA, JAPAN

Inspired by Harry Johnson's Black Thorn Cocktail, my concept was based on a single thought: "Learn a lesson from the past, especially from Dean." Johnson's cocktails characteristically add a few dashes of various liquors. So my cocktail contains dashes of Chartreuse and absinthe. Moreover, my cocktail contains raspberry syrup. In Harry's era, many cocktails were made with raspberry syrup. This cocktail is a congratulatory colour. Always red, not black in 2013, for the great Dean.

Red Thorn Cocktail
45 ml Irish whiskey
30 ml French vermouth
15 ml raspberry syrup
5 ml lemon juice

2 dashes Chartreuse (green)
2 dashes absinthe
Shake up well with shaker, strain into cocktail glass
and serve with lemon twist.

I also love the Bijou Cocktail. Because I like this cocktail's composition. The cocktail is made up of a three-part composition (my opinion): based on spirit (gin), mild bitter (vermouth) and sweet liquor (Chartreuse). Very simple. Good taste. Just like the Negroni.

GIUSEPPE GALLO
LONDON, ENGLAND

Sourcing and researching about vermouth the last few years I had a pleasure to spend a great deal of time with friends of mine (cocktail geeks, or you can call them cocktail historians). I learned so much about gin and vermouth in cocktails as well bartenders' legends about the Dry Martini. Top on my personal list the Marguerite Cocktail, Turf, and Bijou. I decided to combine the several ingredients and make up my very own drink.

H.D.J. Tribute
20 ml London dry gin
30 ml Chartreuse green
10 ml orgeat syrup
15 ml lemon juice
10 ml maraschino liqueur
Shake all ingredients together and double strain in a
flute glass, garnish with float ice chunk.

My favourite Johnson drink is the Coffee Cocktail, an incredible combination of spices, wine and brandy: The ideal drink on a cold winter evening.

SUMIRE MIYANOHARA
TOKYO, JAPAN

The idea for this cocktail is a fusion of Johnson's Bijou Cocktail and his "fountain" technique. I think the Bijou cocktail is an iconic drink in which his fame as a true celebrity bartenders, his success, and his aesthetic sense are all expressed as well as embodying the historical period in which it was created.

In addition, his "fountain" style is still enjoyed by people nowadays and continues to be loved as an icon of how to celebrate a ceremony in style. So, I add history and celebrity to my cocktail, and express that his passion and excellent achievement have definitely been an inspiration for us and have kept shining like "Brilliant Bijous" which in my cocktail is symbolised by the addition of Champagne.

Brilliant Bijous
20 ml Bols Barrel Aged Genever
20 ml Chartreuse Verte V.E.P
20ml Carpano Antica Formula
2 dashes Nord Orange Bitters
1 sugar cube
60 ml Brut Champagne
Layer ingredients except bitters, sugar cube, and Champagne in the following order: Antica Formula, Chartreuse Verte, and Genever. Place the sugar cube on a tray and add the bitters onto the cube. Drop the soaked sugar cube into chilled wine glass

and pour the Champagne and put aside. Pour the
layered ingredients into a mixing glass and stir and
pour into the glass slowly.

The most impressive moment of the Bijou Cocktail is
that I think it really focuses on ladies, the world and the
historical backdrop in which cocktail culture was expanding.

JAMIE BOUDREAU
SEATTLE, WASHINGTON

This drink was inspired by the Fedora, which until I
saw and actually tried the recipe, I would have told anyone
who'd listen that you don't go mixing spirit categories in
a cocktail. Whiskey and rum and cognac?!?! Now I do it
all the time and with more daring combinations that work
(rye and mezcal anyone?). This was one of the first drinks
that made me realize that preconceptions are garbage and
to not be afraid to try anything at least once. It's been many
years since I first came across the Fedora but its lessons
still stick with me, and for that I must tip my hat to Harry
Johnson and the cocktail that first stood out for me in the
Bartenders' Manual.

Cubed Old Fashioned
3/4 oz brandy
3/4 oz rye whiskey
3/4 oz aged rum
1/4 oz old fashioned syrup
1 dash each of aromatic, orange & chocolate bitters
Stir and strain into chilled rocks glass. Garnish with
orange zest.

Old Fashioned Syrup

2 parts sugar
1 part rye
1/4 part Angostura bitters
2 cloves
2 star anise
Put all into pot at medium heat stir until all sugar is
dissolved remove from heat, let cool and bottle.

ADAM EDDY BURSIK
BRATISLAVA, SLOVAKIA

I love the herbal taste and herbal fullness of Harry
Johnson's Bijou Cocktail. This cocktail is about herbs. I
really like the idea to combine the name of cocktail and
ingredients which contain, as well the taste of this cocktail
is very particular for that time when was created, the taste
is seriously "bijou"—old fashioned or rather saying the
sophisticated taste. It's not a cocktail for young people but
for people who knows what they want.

JASON KOSMAS
DALLAS, TEXAS

There a handful of classic cocktails in which the components combine in an orgy of flavours so that you cannot
call out any of the ingredients individually. The Bijou is
such a cocktail. The recipe of gin, Green Chartreuse, sweet
vermouth and orange bitters blend in such harmony that
the sum is greater than its constituents. There is a genius to
this style of cocktail making which Harry Johnson employed
throughout his repertoire.

After opening Employees Only, I became obsessed with conceiving my own 3-ingredient, spirit-driven cocktail made with tequila. Around the same time that I fell in love with Partida Reposado. St-Germain was making waves in cocktail bars everywhere and I was curious how their noses compared and I was struggling for one ingredient to bind them together and create depth.

After being harassed by some young cocktail geeks ordering up round after round of Last Words, it hit me. It was the Green Chartreuse in the Last Word that reminded me of the Bijou cocktail but I would not reach for the green variety but for Yellow Chartreuse. I free-styled this cocktail on the spot using no measurements, only my nose. I called it the Yellow Jacket due to its unique yellow hue and wicked tequila sting. Like the Bijou, this cocktail evolves on the drinker's palate and demands another sip.

Yellow Jacket
2 oz Partida Reposado Tequila
1 oz St-Germain
¾ oz Yellow Chartreuse
1 dash Regan's Orange Bitters
1 Lemon Twist, for garnish
Combine all ingredients into a chilled mixing glass. Add large cold ice and stir until quite chilled. Strain into a chilled cocktail coupe. Garnish with a lemon twist.

ERIK ELLESTAD
SAN FRANCISCO, CA USA

The reason I enjoy Harry Johnson's book so much, is that he was so thorough in documenting and illustrating both his cocktails and the workings of a bar. The illustrations, especially, have proved critical to understanding how late nineteenth-century cocktails were served.

Of the recipes, his Manhattan is maybe my favourite:

Manhattan Cocktail

(Use a large bar glass.)
Fill the glass up with ice;
1 or 2 dashes of gum syrup, very carefully;
1 or 2 dashes of bitters (orange bitters);
1 dash of curaçao or absinthe, if required;
½ wine-glass of whiskey;
½ wine-glass of vermouth;
Stir up well; strain into a fancy cocktail glass;
squeeze a piece of lemon peel on top, and serve;
leave it for the customer to decide, whether to use absinthe or not. This drink is very popular at the present day. It is the bartender's duty to ask the customer, whether he desires his drink dry or sweet.

ERIK LORINCZ
LONDON, ENGLAND

From Johnson I would order his Vermouth Cocktail. I love the simplicity of that drink but in the same time it's such a complex drink with so many layer of flavours.

ANDREA MONTAGUE
LONDON, ENGLAND

I admire Harry Johnson's cocktails for their brilliant simplicity. My favourite being the Marguerite. He uses few ingredients and makes them 'work harder' to achieve extremely elegant beverages.

The Gatsby
40 ml Plymouth gin
20 ml Kamm and Son's—Ginseng Spirit
15 ml Wild nettle cordial
2 dashes Regan's orange bitters
Shake and strain into a cocktail glass.

GAZ REGAN
NEW YORK NY, USA

A tribute to both Johnson and Craddock in the same breath. I think that this is the sort of drink that would please both Harrys. It's elegant, swanky, show-off-y, and really tasty, too.

Am I Blue*
45 ml (1.5 oz) Johnnie Walker Blue Label scotch
15 ml (.5 oz) Noilly Prat sweet vermouth
7.5 ml (.25 oz) Luxardo maraschino liqueur
1 dash Regans' Orange Bitters No. 6
Chilled champagne
1 flamed orange twist, as garnish
Stir the scotch, vermouth, maraschino liqueur, and bitters over ice and strain into a chilled champagne flute. Top with a little chilled champagne and add the garnish.

SIMONE CAPORALE
LONDON, ENGLAND

I fell in love with the Cobbler after reading Harry Johnson's book. I was also inspired when I read Arnaldo Strucchi's 1900 book *Il vermouth di Torino* about the interpretation of Italians' use of vermouth in the US (Johnson's

Vermouth Cocktail; aka: Americano in Italy, adding bitters from Milan to vermouth. Thus I created the Americobbler.

Americobbler

40 ml Martini Rosso
10 ml Cocchi Vermouth di Torino
20 ml Martini Bitter
4 fresh raspberries
1 fresh blackberry
1 slice of lemon
1 slice of orange
1 dash Peychaud's Bitters
1 dash rose water from Lebanon

Muddle all the fruits into a shaker. Add the vermouths and bitters, and rose water. Shake quickly and pour over cracked ice into a medium-size wine glass. Garnish with mint spring, orange slice, mixed berries, silver spoon (for berries) and icing sugar. Serve with straws.

PART TWO

Harry Craddock

CHAPTER TEN

FROM CLOTH TO COCKTAILS

ike Harry "The Dean" Johnson, the life of Harry Craddock—the "Dean of Cocktail Shakers" has been a bit of a mystery to the profession. Some people say he was an American born in Chicago. Some say that he brought cocktails to London. Both statements are far from the truth.

Like Johnson, Craddock contributed a sense of devotion to an industry that he embraced for more than 50 years on two continents. And like Johnson he chronicled a portion of that industry that we now call the "modern age of cocktails" or the dawn of Europe's Golden Age of Cocktails. That's where the similarities end.

Unlike Johnson, Craddock spent only a small portion of his career in the media spotlight. Unlike Johnson, Craddock was a career barman who never ventured into owning his own place or migrating to hotel ownership. From the day he first joined the profession until he retired he was a barman—just a barman. It makes him no less fascinating or important to the bartending pantheon. His is just a another side of a multi-faceted industry.

Born in Burleigh, Minchinhampton in Britain's verdant Cotswolds, on 29 August 1875, Harry Lawson Craddock was the sixth of seven children born to Thomas Henry Craddock and his wife Emma.[36] His father was a tailor from Gloucester and his mother a knitter from Tetbury. The Cotswolds were best known for the dozens of wool market towns such as Minchinhampton, Northleach, Chipping Campden, Chipping Norton, and Burford that sprang up when wool was Britain's gold.

During the Industrial Revolution, Stroud became a cloth town. Textile mills along the rivers churned out yard after yard, mile after mile of woollen cloth, such as the signature Stroudwater Scarlet felt worn by the nation's guardsmen. The Craddock family moved to this weaving centre by 1880, living at 52 High Street.

When Harry finished his studies, the fifteen-year-old worked as a clerk like his older brother Edwin. Yet, six years later he realised he wanted more. He wanted the better life, the opportunities that could possibly be had in America.

When he arrived in New York from Liverpool on 17 March 1897 on board the White Star Lines' *SS Teutonic* he didn't seem to have a specific profession in mind. No one is too sure what sort of jobs he took on as he made his way from Manhattan to Cleveland, Ohio. However, he did end up in one that had experienced a major transformation: bartending.

---

36   Harry's siblings, as recorded when he was 5 years old, included Edwin Daniel (18), Ernest Lewis (15), Annie Mary (13), Edgar Henry (11) Wilfred Edward (9) and baby sister Maud Ellen (1) were living at 36/37 High Street in Stroud.

The bar profession had evolved from an industry of saloon keepers and publicans to bartenders and mixologists in a mere three decades. By the time Craddock landed in New York Jerry "The Professor" Thomas had been in the grave for twelve years, Harry "The Dean" Johnson had moved from bar and café ownership to proprietorship in the hotel industry. "The Only William", Willy Schmidt, held court downtown, wooing the press with his ability to create impromptu drinks with more than a modicum of charm and flair. It looked very appealing to anyone who wanted a high-end service job.

Craddock worked as a waiter at the Hollenden Hotel on Superior and Bond Streets in Cleveland, and shook his very first cocktail because the bartender was not at his post when a customer arrived. The man ordered a Tin Roof Cocktail.

He didn't know what to mix, and the customer gave him step-by-step instructions. Serving it up, Harry asked why it was called a 'tin roof'. The man replied, "because it's on the house." Despite this devious first customer playing a prank that would surface repeatedly in the media from the turn of the century up to the 1920s, when it would finally stop catching even the greenest bartender unaware, Harry was bitten by the bartending bug.

He landed a position as a bartender, on 8 June 1900, at a hotel situated at 219 Ontario Street (which stood on land now occupied by the Cleveland Indians baseball stadium). That job didn't last long. He left for Chicago where he got a post at the Palmer House.

Rebuilt after the 1871 Great Chicago Fire and designed by architect John M Van Osdel, the iron and brick Palmer House was widely advertised as "the world's only fireproof hotel". With oversized rooms, luxurious decor, and sumptuous meals served in grand style, the hotel catered to clients such as US Presidents James Garfield, Grover Cleveland, Ulysses S Grant, William Jennings Bryant, and William McKinley as well as Mark Twain, L Frank Baum, Oscar Wilde, and Sarah Bernhardt. According to Harry, the barbershop floor was tiled with silver dollars. However, Harry didn't last long there because of his inexperience.

Next, he found bartending work on the city's west side. "There, on the first day, the proprietor told him that he had no right to claim to be a first-class bartender with so little experience, but he kept him on, out of admiration for his nerve."

According to a journalist who became a close friend during the 1920s and 1930s, Craddock next found himself in Manhattan and at the Hotel Knickerbocker back in the day when the bartender-turned-hotelier James B Regan opened and managed the property, beginning in 1906, on behalf of owner John Jacob Astor IV.[37] How long Craddock actually stayed there is a mystery.

What is certain is that he went to the majestic Colonial Hotel in Nassau, Grand Bahamas, which had opened in 1900 on the site of Fort Nassau and was in heavy competition for the American tourist trade with rapidly developing south Florida. He worked there until 15 March 1912, then sailed on board the *SS Seguranca* back to New York.

With a good deal of hotel bar experience under his belt, Harry moved to an apartment at 200 East 40th Street in

---

37   You may recall from earlier in this book, Regan collaborated with Captain Frederick Pabst on the Pabst Hotel on 42nd Street before the building was demolished to build the Times Square Terminal and the Times Square Building.

Manhattan. He landed a managerial position in the bar at the Hoffman House, situated at 24th Street and Broadway. He remained there until it closed, in July 1915, to make room for a tall commercial structure.

Opened in 1864, the Hoffman House had been the unofficial annex of Boss Tweed's Tammany Hall which was over on Union Square. The bar had been the training ground for James B Regan before he became a hotelier and was home to an impressive art collection. During the late 1800s, one of its owners, Edward S Stokes, had an eye for art, investing thousands in oil paintings to grace its mahogany walls. He paid $10,010[38] to acquire a single work from 1873 by realist painter Adolph-William Bourguereau: *Nymphs and Satyr.*

Bouguereau's painting graced the bar at the Hoffman House Hotel until 1901 when it was purchased and stored in a warehouse.

---

38   Equivalent to $ 209,105.71 today's currency.

His collection, including Luis Ricardo Falero's haunting *The Vision of Faust* and Antonio Allegri da Correggio's dark fable of *Narcissus*, attracted more than the admiration of gentlemen sippers. Stokes launched a "Ladies Day", during which gentlewomen were escorted by a uniformed attendant to view the collection and receive a printed catalogue.

Newspaper magnate William Randolph Hearst wrote a letter to his mother, while he resided in this hotel, of his intention of owning a New York newspaper. His dream became the stuff of legend.

From there, Harry moved on to another American bartending landmark, the Holland House at 30th Street and Fifth Avenue, where he took a job as bartender. It was while he was there, on 15 September 1916, that he became a naturalised American citizen, something that he expressed his intentions to do when he returned from Nassau five years earlier.

Craddock also finally took time to make a major transition in his personal life.

CHAPTER ELEVEN

ANNIE

merica entered the First World War in April 1917. But that didn't affect Harry as much as making a personal commitment to love. Harry married an Irish widow named Annie Fitzgerald, on 12 June, at St Gabriel's Roman Catholic Church in Manhattan. The daughter of Michael and Annie Broderick, Annie had a child named Louise Emily from her first marriage who had been sent to live with Annie's sister in Cork, Ireland, after the untimely death of Annie's husband Jeremiah.[39] The couple moved into an apartment at 200 West 80th Street at Amsterdam Avenue.

Yet the newly weds could not turn a blind eye to the war. Craddock was still young enough to see service. And as a freshly-minted American citizen he felt that it was his duty to register for the draft. He did so in September 1918. Two months later armistice was called.

With the end of the war, America's sights turned homeward to Prohibition and women's suffrage as key issues in

---

39   Louise Fitzgerald Emily was born 13 January 1904 in New York NY.

the United States Congress. President Woodrow Wilson opposed Prohibition. But both houses fell to the pressure of women's rights lobbyists. The following year was not only a presidential campaign year, but the ratification of the 19th Amendment by Tennessee. The bill was enacted just in time to kick Wilson out of the White House that November.

EXODUS

When Prohibition went into effect, on 16 January 1920, it wasn't as if Americans were oblivious to the fact popular vices were tagged for elimination. The saloons, music clubs, and brothels of San Francisco's Barbary Coast and New Orleans's Storyville were shut down, in 1917, by municipal vice squads in an attempt to clean up their notorious images. New Yorkers knew all too well the battle that raged for a few decades between bar owners and city officials over the increasingly constricting Excise Law.

The Volstead Act itself didn't altogether ban alcohol or stop citizens from drinking it. The bill only prohibited the commercial importation and sale of alcoholic beverages for recreational consumption. Possessing and consuming liquor on private property was not illegal, as long as it had been purchased prior to the passage of the act. Well-off Americans stockpiled private cellars of wines and spirits, both domestic and imported, in their homes and at their private clubs.

Some gentlemen savoured their libations mixed by bartenders who managed to secure employment at elite university clubs, country clubs, hunting clubs. Others enjoyed their cocktails at home, including US President Warren G

Harding, who kept a supply of booze in the White House during his administration.

But for Harry Craddock, Prohibition meant the end of a career that he had built for himself. Reputedly shaking the "last legal cocktail to be served in New York" on that fateful day in January 1920, Harry found himself jobless, supporting a wife and a sixteen-year-old step-daughter who had come to live with them only four months earlier. It was time to head to the greener pastures of home.

Craddock applied for an American passport, and on 27 April 1920, he and his family arrived in Liverpool on board the White Star Line's *SS The Baltic*. Describing himself as being in the hotel business, Craddock gave their destination address as Devonshire Road, where his older brother Ernest resided.

1920: Harry and Annie Craddock along with Louise Emily Fitzgerald as they appeared in their passport application.

As an insurance policy, Harry included Annie on his American passport and gave his legal residence as their New York apartment. In truth, he seriously hoped that Prohibition would end quickly so he could return to the country that offered him a position in life in an honourable profession. He told American embassy officials that he was only visiting relatives for health reasons. In truth, he had moved the family to 10 Pembridge Crescent, Notting Hill, and was job hunting.

REGAN RETIRES

James B Regan also left America when Prohibition began. Gone were the days of working behind the bar at the Hoffman House, owning a healthy chunk of the Pabst Hotel and the Woodmansten Inn, as well as managing Astor's Hotel Knickerbocker. Regan had also made a fortune importing wine and cigars as well as delving into other investments. He had put his son James Jr through Yale University.

When his daughter became Mrs William Gardener and moved to London with her British diplomat husband, the Regans followed her. James purchased a mansion not far from the home of American Ambassador Colonel George Harvey. The retired couple divided their time amongst New York, London, and continental Europe.

Known for his generous nature, James Regan never forgot the early days when he was a young bar-boy, scrubbing bottles behind the bar at Old Earle's Hotel for practically nothing. During the brutal winters of 1915 and 1916, when the unemployed froze and starved in city parks, his "bread line" at the rear of the Hotel Knickerbocker kept the less-fortunate fed night and day. Was it possible that Harry contacted his former employer when he arrived in London in hopes of getting a foot into a door?

As one article noted, in 1930: "Every year [Harry] renews acquaintanceship with old friends of his New York days, and he probably knows as many eminent men on both sides of the Atlantic as any other man living." He needed all the help he could get to land the right job, or rather any job.

THE COCKTAIL OFFENSIVE

Reports from London, in 1905, indicated that "every attempt to maintain a high-class American bar in London has failed. The latest proof of this is furnished by the transference of the Criterion's American bar, long the most famous feature of that popular Piccadilly resort, to another and less conspicuous part of the building, where, dwarfed in size and shorn of its former glory, it probably will continue to make a feeble struggle for existence a few years longer."

When interviewed about this shift in trend, the Criterion's Austrian-born manager explained:

> It is because in London Americans seem to prefer adhering to the old adage which bids them when in Rome to do as Romans do. Taking the resident and floating American population together, there are enough of them to keep several American bars and restaurants going. But they won't give them enough of their patronage to make them pay. And though in America the Englishman displays all the zeal of the convert in his appreciation of American mixed drinks and bestows a more guarded approval on American dishes, on his

native heath he seems to regard it as a patriotic duty to set himself sternly against any innovations in the matter of food and liquors.

The manager also noted that:

> There is no doubt, too, that the American bar in London has suffered grievously in reputation because of the many spurious imitations of it that have been foisted on the public.

Based on that assessment, it's no wonder that Londoners feared cocktails after experiencing the offerings of the time. And it's no wonder that more than one well-heeled American offered hard cash to any one who could find a "genuine American bartender—one who had been born in the United States and had learned the art of mixing drinks there—now dispensing American drinks in London."

True. There were personal valets and butlers who were well versed in making proper cocktails thanks to enthusiastic, rich employers who could afford to arrange for private tutors like Harry Johnson to teach them the fine art of mixing cocktails, American style. But the average citizen was subjected to high-street versions rather than high-end.

This made a return to Britain no bed of roses for Harry. Fifteen years after the American drinks trend waned an editorial comment appeared in a 1920 edition of *Catering Industry Employee* magazine:

> THE COCKTAIL IN LONDON. It is said that the cocktail offensive in London has failed, that the Englishman still sticks to the supping of his whisky and soda, instead of dashing off the 'dum-dum' of gin and

vermouth. Perhaps the advance of the cocktail has been checked in London. That great American exile among potations may not yet have broken through the phlegm of the Englishman. But the check is only temporary.

Craddock threw in his glove, writing an op-ed piece that was published in the *Daily Express*:

> When I write that I know that I am inviting controversy, but I think I can prove my statement by facts. The young man of to-day is told by most old men to be incapable of judgement in food and wine, and by others, such as Sir Claude Champion de Crespigny [4th Baronet], to be 'degenerate'.
>
> One does not drink a cocktail merely to mollify thirst any more than one merely wears clothes to keep warm. The object of a true cocktail, when created by an artist is that it shall give point and piquancy to that meal of which it is the forerunner. In addition to this a properly mixed cocktail cleans the throat, facilitates the digestion, and improves the liver and the stomach.
>
> There is no doubt whatsoever and I have the authority of great doctors and surgeons on this matter, that the cocktail is of considerable value to digestion and, on the other hand, drinks of our grandfather's 'home-brewed ale in a cool earthen pot' or a whisky and soda are terrible things to take before a meal. They unbalance the stomach, carry no lightness or assistance to the digestive organs or to the liver, and spoil the appetite.
>
> Bad cocktails are like bad wine for fools or the unlucky and we must except these.
>
> A cocktail is no more a "craze" than soup or fish which is enjoyed every night.

I do not know whether we should thank the United States for cocktails or not.

Permit me to argue, forbidding old gentlemen, these cocktails were not invented five years ago, but thirty-five years ago, when they were young men and that they are no more a sign of degeneration that any other drink equally healthful, harmless, and beneficial to the digestion and the stomach.

For health's sake drink cocktails!

It is obvious from this letter that rather than admit immediate defeat in the face of such apathy, Harry set out to champion the American cocktail in his homeland.

OF BRITISH ORIGIN

It wasn't that cocktails were unknown in London, let alone Great Britain. Until very recently, the earliest-known use of the word "cocktail" in print that referenced drink was in 1806 in an upstate New York newspaper. Then in 2005, it was discovered in an 1803 Vermont newspaper. Two years ago we found the word employed on 20 March 1798, in *The Morning Post and Gazetteer*, a long-defunct London newspaper. The paper had reported, on 16 March, that the landlord of the Axe & Gate Tavern at the corner of Downing and Whitehall, on winning a share of a lottery, returned to his establishment and erased his regulars' scores with a mop "in a transport of joy".

Four days later the paper printed a satirical article listing who owed for what drinks in the heart of British politics. A certain Mr Rose (while writing letters upon the reform of public offices) owed for "gin and bitters". Another owed for

35 nips of "glue", "commonly called Burton ale, to make the members of the neutrality stick together".

Toward the bottom, William Pitt the younger, whose premiership was witness to the French Revolution and would soon be marked by the Napoleonic Wars, owed for "L'huile de Venus", "perfait [sic] amour", and a less French drink: "'cock-tail' (vulgarly called ginger)."

Exactly what this implied is open to conjecture. The most common use of the term "cocktail" at the time was in reference to a horse with its tail cut short to indicate it was a mixed breed. One colic remedy found in veterinary manuals from the period blended water, oats, gin, and ginger.

Gingering was a technique employed by horse traders to fetch higher prices for their cocktails. A horse with a spring in its step, wide-open eyes, and most importantly tail held high would sell for more. A well-placed knob of peeled ginger did the trick, at least until the horse was sold. Considering Pitt had recently doubled the price of the paper with a tax (the masthead read "price 3d, taxed by Mr. Pitt 3d, total 6d") the newspaper's editor could have been suggesting either one.

Jerry "The Professor" Thomas, the Connecticut native who in 1862 wrote the first known book to contain a section of cocktail recipes, is considered by many to be the father of modern bartending. The purely American father. However, he actually worked in London prior to penning this pioneering tome.

It appears that he or someone very much like him interviewed for a job, around 1851, at French chef Alexis Benoit Soyer's Universal Symposium of All Nations where the Albert Hall now stands. Soyer's American bar—aptly named The Washington Refreshment Room—was London's first American bar when it opened, in 1851, and boasted forty drinks on its menu ranging from Shandygaffs, Mint Juleps, Hailstorms, Brandy Smashes, and Soyer's own Nectar Cobblers. The famed chef hired a barman from West London instead of the American who professed that he was "perfectly capable of compounding four at a time, swallowing a flash of lightning, smoking a cigar, singing *Yankee Doodle*, washing up the glasses, and performing the overture to the *Huguenots* on the banjo simultaneously."

But Thomas wound up serving the flux of unfortunate ladies and the Pre-Raphaelites who loved them in the American Bowling Saloon that stood at the heart of the Cremorne Pleasure Gardens in Chelsea. Even so, Soyer's influence was undeniable. Thomas's documentation, in 1862, of Soyer's drink recipes illustrate the influence of the Reform Club's founding chef, the world's first celebrity chef, and early "fancy drink" pioneer had on this legendary father of modern bartending.

Here are three examples from his 1862 book *How to Mix Drinks, Or The Bon-Vivant's Companion*:

11. Gin Punch

(From a recipe by Soyer.)
½ pint of old gin
1 gill of maraschino
The juice of two lemons
The rind of half a lemon
Four ounces of syrup
1 quart bottle of German Seltzer water
Ice well.

171. Balaklava Nectar. (By Soyer.)

(For a party of fifteen.)

Thinly peel the rind of half a lemon, shred it fine,
and put it in a punch-bowl ; add two table-spoon-
fuls of crushed sugar, and the juice of two lemons,
the half of a small cucumber sliced thin, with the
peel, on ; toss it up several times, then add 2 bottles
of soda-water, 2 of claret, 1 of champagne, stir well
together, and serve.

172. Crimean Cup, & la Marmora.

(From a recipe by the celebrated Soyer.)

(For a party of thirty.)

1 quart of syrup of orgeat.

1 pint of Cognac brandy.

½ do. maraschino.

½ do. Jamaica rum.

2 bottles of champagne.

2 do. soda-water.

6 ounces of sugar.

4 middling-sized lemons.

Thinly peel the lemons, and place the rind in a bowl
with the sugar, macerate them well for a minute or
two, in order to extract the flavour from the lemon.
Next squeeze the juice of the lemons upon this, add
two bottles of soda-water, and stir well till the sugar
is dissolved; pour in the syrup of orgeat, and whip
the mixture well with an egg- whisk, in order to
whiten the composition. Then add the brandy, rum
and maraschino, strain the whole into the punch-
bowl, and just before serving add the champagne,
which should be well iced. While adding the champagne, stir well with the ladle; this will render the
cup creamy and mellow.

It's worth noting that the first bar serving American
drinks in England wasn't in London at all, but appropriately

in a port city. Up in Liverpool, in 1844, savvy hotel owners capitalised on the recent availability of commercial ice from New England and Norway, offering guests Sherry Cobblers, Mint Juleps, and other "American drinks" because "the icehouse is peculiarly adapted for the immediate supply."[40]

WHITEMAN'S
BRUNSWICK HOTEL AND RESTAURANT,
HANOVER-STREET, LIVERPOOL,
Five Minutes' walk from the Railway and Exchange.

W. E. WHITEMAN has the pleasure to inform his Friends and the Public at large, that, in order to render his Establishment worthy of the patronage he has so long received, he has completed alterations more conducive to the comfort of his Guests, by Enlarging his
COFFEE-ROOM AND RESTAURANT, and will be found *at home* in the Culinary Department, which will combine ECONOMY with DESPATCH.
The Icehouse is peculiarly adapted for the immediate supply of SHERRY COBLERS, MINT JULEPS, and other American Drinks; also a choice Vintage of CRUSTED PORT and PALE SHERRY, in Half-pint Bottles.
W. E. W. has a large Room suitable for Commercial Gentlemen, Clubs, and Dinner Parties.
A supply of GAME, TURTLE, and VENISON.

1844: This advertisement attests to the fact that interest in iced "American drinks" went beyond London, all the way north to Liverpool.

As the United States grew prosperous, the number of American tourists visiting London swelled. The few "American Bars" that had cropped up were seeing enough business to spawn a trend in cocktail joints. The young British barkeepers working in them quickly grasped the air of creativity and birthed countless new drinks. Many of these found their way to the States, only to be introduced to Europe a few years later as genuine American drinks.

In 1869, the first British book containing cocktail recipes was published: William Terrington's *Cooling Cups and Dainty Drinks*. Reaching back to that first use of the word

---

40   Advertisement. Liverpool Mercury 6 september 1844

"cocktail", his first recipe was for a Gin Cocktail made with brandy or gin, ginger syrup, aromatic bitters, and a splash of water. (Terrington's book sported a back cover advertisement for the Wenham Lake Ice Company, which imported New England ice and distributed it with ice chests throughout London for a subscription fee.)

New York transplant Leo Engel took the reins of the American bar at The Criterion on Piccadilly Circus a decade later, publishing his own slim volume of recipes, *American and Other Drinks*. But it wasn't until another French chef and a famed hotelier collaborated on a luxury hotel project that London had a temple of cocktails on par with Holland House, Hoffman House, and other American drinking landmarks.

Petite and pretty, Ada Coleman graced the bars at both Claridge's and the Savoy's American bar for more than two decades.

CHAPTER TWELVE

ADA

orn near Villeneuve-Loubet, Georges Auguste Escoffier was one of those lucky souls who was born at the right time and put himself in the right place. Creator of gastronomic delights such as Tournedos Rossini and Pêche Melba, Escoffier elevated the art of cooking to a revered profession throughout Europe. Together with hotel manager César Ritz, in 1890, Escoffier opened Richard D'Oyly Carte's Savoy Hotel on the Strand. (D'Oyly Carte made a fortune producing the operettas of WS Gilbert and Arthur Sullivan as well as owning the Savoy Theatre.) When the Savoy reopened after its retrofit, in 1898, it sported an American bar with Frank Wells as its first head barman.

D'Oyly Carte also purchased Claridge's Hotel, in 1893, rebuilt it from the ground up. Reopening, in 1898, it also featured an American bar in its renovation. But it also possessed a very unusual touch: a barmaid named Ada Coleman.

Ada Coleman. Anyone versed with London's cocktail history or the story of the Savoy hotel will know Coley as the Savoy's first female bartender.

However, she wasn't.

Ada's was a Cinderella story. Her first job at Claridge's was not in the bar, but in the flower shop making "button-holes"—miniature flower arrangements—for gentlemen to wear on their lapels. Her move to the bar there brought her into contact with a man named Fisher, a wine merchant who supplied the hotel. It was Fisher who, as Ada would recall years later, first taught her how to handle a shaker and mix a cocktail. The her knight in shining armour, Rupert D'Oyly Carte whisked her away to the Savoy to take up a position behind the bar in the newly-renovated property.

Coley arrived with a head full of new drinks and a powerful charm that launched her toward immortality. There, she started working with Ruth Burgess. The press dubbed them Miss B and Coley. Later they were named Kitty and Coley.

> The bar was opened in 1902 by Miss Burgess, familiarly known as 'Miss B', who then—the old-timers say—was a tall, slim girl," one news report explained. "Shortly afterwards 'Coley' came, short and pretty, with laughing eyes and a ready wit.'Coley' brought some cocktail receipts of her own, which were new in those infant days of the art of cocktail mixing. That speedily caused the quarrel. Customers liked Coley's cocktails and asked for them when Coley was off duty. Miss B didn't know how to mix them. She asked Coley to give her the ingredients, and Coley, with perhaps justifiable professional pride refused.

From that day forward, Kitty and Coley never spoke again for twenty years. Both happily greeted their patrons and pleasantly bantered with them as they made drinks. But both refused to acknowledge the other's existence if they worked the same shift. Ada got occasional offers to tend bar in America, but she refused to leave her beloved London or her station at the American Bar.

Coley became the bar's media darling, especially when she created the Hanky Panky Cocktail for Sir Charles Hawtrey. Coleman herself recalled that:

> The late Charles Hawtrey... was one of the best judges of cocktails that I knew. Some years ago, when he was overworking, he used to come into the bar and say, 'Coley, I am tired. Give me something with a bit of punch in it.' It was for him that I spent hours experimenting until I had invented a new cocktail. The next time he came in, I told him I had a new drink for him. He sipped it, and, draining the glass, he said, 'By Jove! That is the real hanky-panky!' And Hanky-Panky it has been called ever since.

Hanky Panky Cocktail
2 dashes Fernet Branca
1 part Italian vermouth
1 part dry gin
Shake well and strain into cocktail glass. Squeeze
orange peel on top.

Despite the fact that Ruth Burgess had seniority, Ada's popularity made everyone assume that she was the head bartender, even when Harry applied for a job.

He was hired to work the Savoy's dispensary bar, on 20 September 1921, and although she didn't know it, Harry's acquired American accent and American passport, plus his American bar training positioned him to be the poster child for American drinks in London. Almost as soon as he put his bar kit own, Harry started inventing drinks, some to commemorate local events.

With the 1923 success of Leon Gordon's play *White Cargo* in the West End's theatre district, Harry came up with a simple yet insidious concoction by the same name. And he was just getting started.

The White Cargo
1 part French vanilla ice cream
1 part gin
No ice is necessary; just shake until thoroughly mixed, and add cold water or white wine, if the concoction is too thick.

A 20 March 1923 notice on the International News Service read: "The cocktail season is about to open and Harry Craddock the 'cocktail king' has gone into training." The item went on to say that Craddock boasted of mixing at least 100,000 cocktails for the Savoy's American guests and a few thousand more for "visitors of other nationalities." Apparently, Craddock worked out at least two weeks before the season, trained at the gym for three hours in the morning and three hours in the afternoon just so he could be in peak condition to hold his shaker high.

He wasn't the only one taking exercise. The next year, it was noted that:

> The new Lord Mayor of London [Sir Alfred Bower of Bower & Company, Wine Merchants] is undergoing a tremendous ordeal. For the first eight weeks of his administration there is not a single day on which he has neither a banquet or a luncheon engagement. To

offset this his physicians have ordered that he shall exercise daily. ... Although the Lord Mayor is himself a wine merchant, occasionally on his daily walk he slips into the Thames Embankment entrance of the Savoy to sample one of Harry Craddock's American cocktails.

American writers, artists, and musicians headed to Europe in hopes of finding intellectual freedom. Europe called on American mixologists, too. Someone had to make cocktails for Britain's devil-may-care Bright Young Things and their chroniclers Noël Coward, Evelyn Waugh, and PG Wodehouse, who frequented London's Café Royal, Ciro's Club, and the Savoy.

3rd June 1926: Craddock expertly mixes a drink as the head barman in the Savoy's American bar. (Photo by Topical Press Agency/Getty Images)

November 1927: Writers and brothers Osbert and Sacheverell Sitwell observe the Savoy Hotel's Martyn Roland and Harry Craddock how to shake a cocktail. (Photo by Fox Photos/Getty Images)

Year after year, Prohibition changed the face of drinking not only in America, but across the Atlantic as thirsty tourists arrived in London in droves. The city's Bright Young Things dubbed the Savoy's American Bar the "49th State of the USA" because of its growing US clientele. However, Americans—New Yorkers especially—felt it was inappropriate for women to work in bar rooms. (Even Willy "The Only William" Schmidt retired from the bar because he refused to work behind the mahogany with a woman.)

To them, barmaids were a strictly British phenomena, and not an acceptable one at the time. Was it in keeping with the customers' preferences, Rupert D'Oyly Carte let

Kitty and Coley retire, on 17 December 1925, and promoted Harry Craddock to head barman?

A month later, Ada was at the Savoy's flower shop, commenting in an interview that: "I should have missed all my friends too much if I had retired at once, so I've come to work among the flowers, and already instead of mixing cocktails for my friends, I've been making buttonholes for them."

There is no question Harry's star rose meteorically. By 1927, he was promoted as a celebrity on a higher level than many of the film and theatrical stars as well as nobles that he served. In early November of that year, Madame Tussaud's unveiled a wax figure of him in its London museum.

Barkeep
Now Immortal in Waxworks.

Mme. T. Tussaud's famous waxworks have been revived in London and one of the new exhibits is a life-sized effigy of Harry Craddock, "the last American bartender to mix a cocktail." He is shown shaker in hand and apron gracefully draped across his mid-section.

The public has always had great faith in waxworks, but its credulity will be shaken by this exhibit. Photographs can't lie, of course, but waxworks, apparently, are different.

The "last American bartender to shake a cocktail" has not yet shaken it. Thousands of them are shaking cocktails every day. Why mislead the British that way?

An item that appeared in the Syracuse Journal on 8 November 1927, announcing the unveiling of Craddock's wax figure at Madam Tussaud's in London.

He had become close friends with a few influential writers and American journalists. Though a few papers

reported that he did not drink one journalist, New York's
Evening World and *New York Sun* columnist—and frequent
Savoy patron—Karl K Kitchen, devoted an entire syndicated
column to a drinking round in the Savoy with Harry, while
they chatted about concerts:

> "Is that you, Oswald?" (Mr Manhattan always
> calls me Oswald because my name is Karl) came a
> cheery familiar voice from the next room."
> "Certainly not," I sang back as I slipped out of
> my overcoat.
> "Cut the comedy and fanny yourself into the
> Bad Boy's Den," came the response. And as soon as
> Chaucer [Harry's assistant] had my coat I pushed down
> the hall to the library, where I found my old friend in
> the delightful act of shaking a cocktail.

Harry offered Kitchen a Blue Train Cocktail, a variation
on the White Lady, pouring one for each of them.

Blue Train Cocktail
¼ Lemon Juice
¼ Cointreau
½ Dry Gin
1 Dash Blue Vegetable Extract
Shake well and strain to cocktail glass.

When Kitchen asked if there was an appropriate toast
for the drink, Harry replied: "Here's to Hades! May our stay
there be as pleasant as our way there." They then proceeded
to get a few rounds in, mixed by Chaucer. However, Harry
was still as focused as ever.

A MOMENT IN TIME

Streamline, sleek, geometric. Art Deco was all the rage amongst those in the know during the 1920s and 1930s. And far be it that the Savoy was going to lag behind when it came to fashion or trend. The American Bar was redesigned to reflect this new style. But before the familiar "jazz age" design was set in place, Craddock placed a White Lady Cocktail in a cocktail shaker as a time capsule that was bricked up into one of the walls. (When the hotel was closed in December 2007 for a complete refitting, staff looked for the time capsule shaker, but it was never located.)

1927: Craddock buried a shaker containing a White Lady cocktail within the walls of the rebuilt American Bar at the Savoy (Photo: Savoy Group archives)

PRW15

The Management has secured the services of a leading Cocktail Expert from the U.S.A.
The following are a few of the drinks selected from a list of 200 :—

COCKTAILS.

Savoy Hotel Special No. 1	2/–
Appetizer No. 1.	2/–
East & West	2/–
Hankey-Pankey	2/–
Lutkins Special	2/–
Martini (Dry or Sweet)	2/–
Manhattan (Dry or Sweet)	2/–
Orange Blossom	2/–
Old Fashion	2/–
Rob Roy	2/–
Sonora	2/–
Waldorf Astoria	2/–
Bronx	2/–
do. Silver	2/6
Bacardi	2/6
Bentley	2/6
Clover Club	2/6
Cuban	2/6
Dacqueri	2/6
Doctor	2/6
Favorite	2/6
Hesitation	2/6
Jack Rose	2/6
Millionaire	2/6
Monkey Gland	2/6
Paradise	2/6
Resolute	2/6
Royal Smile	2/6
Star	2/6
Side Car	2/6
White Lady	2/6

COOLERS (long drinks).

Savoy Hotel Special	2/6
Sherry Cobbler	2/6
Tom Collins	2/6
London Buck	2/6
Leap Frog	2/6
Mamie Taylor	2/6
Southern Mint Julep	2/6

LIQUEURS.

Savoy Hotel Special	3/–
Maiden's Dream	3/–
Pousse Café	3/–
Diana	2/6
Princess	2/6
Angel's Tip	2/6
Angel's Wing	2/6
Fifth Avenue	2/6
Broadway Smile	2/6
Sunrise	2/6

DAISIES.

Savoy Hotel Special	2/6
Gin	2/6
Rum	2/6

FIZZES.

Savoy Hotel Special	2/–
Gin	2/–
Sloe Gin	2/6
Silver	2/6
Golden	2/6
Royal	2/6
Grand Royal	2/6
Morning Glory	2/6

FLIPS.

Savoy Hotel Special	2/6
Sherry	2/6
Coffee	2/6
Port	2/6

SOURS.

Savoy Hotel Special	2/6
Rum	2/6
Whisky	2/6

5-1-28

1928: The January cocktail menu at the American Bar.

COCKTAILS		COCKTAILS—(continued)		COCKTAILS—(continued)	
Savoy Hotel Special No. 1	2/-	Duke of Marlborough	2/-	Old Fashioned Rye...	2/-
,, ,, ,, No. 2	2/-	Elk	2/-	,, ,, Bourbon	2/-
Affinity	2/-	Fairy Belle	2/-	,, ,, Scotch	2/-
After Dinner	2/6	Favorite	2/6	,, ,, Gin ...	2/-
Alexandra	2/6	Fifty-Fifty	2/-	,, ,, Toddy	2/-
Allies	2/-	Froth Blower	2/-	,, ,, Brandy	2/6
Appetizer No. 1	2/-	Gibson	2/-	Panama	2/-
,, No. 2	2/-	Gin	2/-	Paradise	2/6
Bacardi	2/6	Hankey-Pankey	2/-	Perfect	2/-
Bamboo	2/-	H.P.W.	2/-	Picon	2/-
Barney French	2/-	Harvard	2/6	Polo	2/-
Bentley	2/6	Hercules	2/6	Poppy	2/-
Blue Monday	2/6	Hesitation	2/6	President	2/-
Blue Train...	2/6	Hildebrand	2/-	Queen	2/-
Brandy	2/6	Ideal	2/6	Racquet Club	2/-
Brain Storm	2/6	Imperial	2/-	Raymond Hitchcocktail	2/-
Bronx	2/-	Jack Rose	2/6	Resolute	2/6
,, (Crystal)	2/-	Kina Lillet	2/-	Rob Roy	2/-
,, (Silver)	2/6	Leave it to Me	2/-	Royal Smile	2/6
Caperitif	2/6	Lone Tree	2/-	Salome	2/-
Casino	2/-	Lutkins Special	2/-	Santiago	2/-
Champagne Cocktails	3/6	McNish	2/-	Sazerac	2/-
Clover Leaf	2/6	Mayor Osgood	2/-	Shamrock IV.	2/-
,, Club	2/6	Manhattan (Dry)	2/-	Side Car	2/6
Cooperstown	2/-	,, (Sweet)...	2/-	Snake in the Grass	2/6
Coronation...	2/-	,, C. C.	2/-	Sonora	2/-
Cuban	2/6	Martini (Dry)	2/-	Star	2/6
Dacqueri	2/6	,, (Sweet)	2/-	Stinger	2/6
Depth Charge	2/6	Merry Widow	2/-	Turf	2/-
Doctor	2/6	Millionaire	2/6	Waldorf-Astoria	2/-
Dubonnet	2/-	Monkey Gland	2/6	White Lady	2/6
Duchess	2/6	Orange Blossom	2/-	Zaza	2/-

1929: Page one of the expanded American Bar menu.

It goes without saying that not all the recipes that Harry mixed were of his invention. Many came from the people who visited him at the bar. "Every year I have from twelve to twenty new cocktail recipes brought to me by American friends," he admitted. "America is still the spiritual home of the cocktail, and the elderly American is still the best critic of a cocktail. There is, too, the American who thinks of a new cocktail at home and brings the recipe to Europe to be materialised, because he cannot get the required ingredients. Many a pilgrim does that."

Armed with an index box filled cocktail recipes, Craddock made the news again when, in the first week of October 1928, he added the 2000th formula to his bursting arsenal. As a major marketing promotion, hotel management asked him to compile his library into a single volume. *The Savoy Cocktail Book* was published by Constable & Company Ltd in 1930 to great fanfare, especially as Craddock had endeared himself to Britain's jazz-loving, American-centric Bright Young Things.

Containing over 1,000 cocktails and mixed drinks, Craddock's compendium differed from his esteemed predecessor Harry Johnson's work in many ways. Where Johnson focused on bar operations and ownership as well as a few hundred popular drinks of the day, Craddock devoted his work to presenting cocktails and mixed drinks that fell into three categories: enduring classics, popular orders placed at the Savoy, scatterings of good humour, and of course, his own creations.

Corpse Reviver No 2

¼ Wine Glass Lemon Juice
¼ Wine Glass Kina Lillet
¼ Wine Glass Cointreau
¼ Wine Glass Dry Gin
1 Dash absinthe
Shake well and strain into cocktail glass.
Four of these taken in swift succession will unrevive
the corpse again.

Harry's Cocktail

1/3 Gancia Italian Vermouth
1 Dash Absinthe
2/3 Gin
2 Sprigs of Fresh Mint
Shake well and strain into cocktail glass. Serve with
a stuffed olive.

Leap Year Cocktail

1 Dash Lemon Juice
2/3 Gin
1/6 Grand Marnier
1/6 Italian Vermouth
Shake well and strain into cocktail glass. Squeeze
lemon peel on top.
This cocktail was created by Harry Craddock for
the Leap year celebrations at the Savoy Hotel,
London, on February 29th 1928. It is said to have
been responsible for more proposals than any other
cocktail that has ever been mixed.

Princess Mary's Pride Cocktail

¼ French Vermouth
¼ Dubonnet
½ Calvados
Shake well and strain into cocktail glass.

Created by Harry Craddock on February 28, 1922,
to mark the wedding celebrations of HRH Princess
Mary.

Strike's Off Cocktail

¼ Lemon or Lime Juice
¼ Swedish Punch
½ Gin
Shake well and strain into cocktail glass.
Created by Harry Craddock on May 12, 1926, to
mark the end of the General Strike.

White Lady Cocktail

¼ Lemon Juice
¼ Cointreau
½ Dry Gin
Shake well and strain into cocktail glass.

Paying homage to the three hotel bars in which he learned
his skills, Harry included the Hoffman House Cocktail, the
Holland House Cocktail, and the Knickerbocker Cocktail.

Hoffman House Cocktail

2 Dashes Orange Bitters
1/3 French Vermouth
2/3 Plymouth Gin
Shake well and strain into cocktail glass. Squeeze
lemon peel on top.

Holland House Cocktail

The Juice of ¼ Lemon
1 Slice Pineapple
1/3 French Vermouth
2/3 Dry Gin
4 Dashes Maraschino
Shake well and strain into cocktail glass.

Knickerbocker Cocktail
1 Dash Italian Vermouth
1/3 French Vermouth
2/3 Dry Gin
Shake well and strain into cocktail glass. Squeeze
lemon peel on top.

A few of the transformations that the cocktail had experienced just as Prohibition shifted attention from America to other ports such as Cuba were also chronicled. Exposed to the first wave of interest in Cuban cocktails when he was in New York—as were most of his American patrons—he included his personal take on drinks such as the Maragato Cocktail (Special). Originally created by Spanish-born barman Emilio "Maragato" González when he presided at Havana's Hotel Florida and Hotel Plaza, Craddock opted the orange juice for lemon and lime as well as adding a dash of kümmel.

Maragato Cocktail (Special)
1/3 Bacardi Rum
1/3 French Vermouth
1/3 Italian Vermouth
1 Dash Kirsch
The Juice of ½ Lemon
The Juice of 1/3 Lime
A little sugar dissolved in soda-water.
Shake well and strain into cocktail glass.

Tequila was exported as far as Europe in Harry's day, but was not always readily available. Consequently a drink named after a Mexican desert region—the Sonora Cocktail—was documented as containing rum. Try it with tequila, Harry did. This drink made its public debut on 21 August 1925, in the *Western Daily Press*, a Bristol, England newspaper. There, it called for "tequila, which is extracted from the Mexican cactus".

Sonora Cocktail
1 Dash Lemon Juice
2 Dashes Apricot brandy
½ Applejack or Calvados
½ Bacardi Rum
Shake well and strain into cocktail glass.

Another new spirit to enter the bar was vodka. And Harry's Russian Cocktail was a premonition of things to come more than a half century later.

Russian Cocktail
1/3 Crème de Cacao
1/3 Dry Gin
1/3 Vodka
Shake well and strain into cocktail glass, and tossitoff quickski.

Where Ada Coleman had a soft spot for Fernet Branca, Craddock's heart warmed at the sight of Kina Lillet, or simply Lillet–so much so that he crafted a series of original recipes for the company, which it published as a promotional brochure. He also added them to *The Savoy Cocktail Book*.

The Abbey
¾ Lillet
¼ Italian Vermouth
4 Dashes Lemon Juice
Shake and serve cold with a French olive on a wooden stick.

Depth Charge
2 Dashes Absinthe
½ Wine Glass Lillet
½ Wine Glass London Dry Gin
Squeeze orange peel on top.

Green Eye
¾ Lillet
¼ Crème de Menthe Syrup (green)
4 Dashes Orange Bitters
Shake and serve cold with a Maraschino cherry on a
wooden stick.

Lindbergh
2 Dashes Orange Juice
2 Dashes Apricot Brandy
½ Wine Glass Lillet
½ Wine Glass Plymouth Gin
Squeeze lemon peel on top.

Lillet Cocktail
2 dashes Orange Bitters
2/3 Lillet
1/3 Dry Gin
Shake well and serve cold.

Lillet Special
¾ Lillet
¼ Campari Bitters
4 Dashes Orange Juice
Shake and serve cold with a Maraschino cherry on a
wooden stick.

Old Etonian
2 Dashes Orange Bitters
2 Dashes Crème de Noyaux

½ Wine Glass London Dry Gin
½ Wine Glass Lillet
Squeeze orange peel on top.

Self Starter

1/8 Wine Glass Apricot Brandy
2/8 Wine Glass Lillet
½ Wine Glass London Dry Gin
2 Dashes Absinthe

Sunshine

½ Wine Glass Lillet
½ Wine Glass French Vermouth
4 Dashes Orange Juice
Shake and serve with a small piece of orange peel in
the glass.

With the publication of *The Savoy Cocktail Book*, Harry's name became a household word. Some reporters called him "The Dean of the Cocktail Shakers". Karl K Kitchen referred to him as "Mr Manhattan" when he chronicled Craddock's creativity more than once even before the book was published in his syndicated "Man About Town" and "A Broadwayite in Ireland" columns:

Yesterday I asked Harry Craddock to invent a new cocktail for me. Instead, he invented three. At noon today, when I paid my daily visit, he gave me three recipes with the suggestion I should name the one I liked best 'Mr Manhattan'. However, all three are so excellent and are made of ingredients so easily obtainable in America, that I will give the recipes for the benefit of those who want something new.
I quote him verbatim:

Mr Manhattan No 1—Crush one lump of sugar in a little water; then crush four leaves of fresh green mint; one dash of lemon juice; four dashes of orange juice; gin.

Mr Manhattan No. 2—Saturate a lump of sugar with raspberry syrup or grenadine; one-third vermouth; two-thirds hooch whisky.

Mr Manhattan No. 3—One-quarter white grape juice; four dashes grenadine; three-fourths Scotch whisky.

In another encounter, Craddock mixed the admiring journalist his Prohibition Cocktail:

Craddock did not hesitate for a moment. He reached for two or three bottles, poured some of their contents into a shaker and after a few genuflections squeezed a little lemon peel over the concoction with filled the glass he put out for me.

'This should inspire the best and highest feelings,' he said, adding 'without unduly raising your hopes or letting you down with a bang.'

Prohibition Cocktail
2 Dashes Orange Juice
1 Dash Apricot Brandy
½ Kina Lillet
½ Plymouth Gin
Shake well and strain into cocktail glass. Squeeze lemon peel on top.

Not everyone in Britain was enamoured with cocktails and the recent rise in their popularity amongst Londoners, let alone Harry's popularity in the press because of them. The president of the Society for the Study of Inebriety, Sir

Arthur Newsholme, in giving evidence to the Royal Commission on Licensing, in 1930, commented in the strongest terms that "I am against the cocktail; it is a very bad habit." In an open letter addressed to the editor of the *Daily Express*, Craddock defended the cocktail's honour:

> Presumably, therefore, Sir Arthur would prohibit the cocktail—with what result? ...I defend the cocktail. There is good in it where it is treated as it should be, like all other things which go to make life a little smoother, sanely and with common sense as the majority of cocktail drinkers do treat it.

Harry returned to the United States, that year, the first time in a deacde. Before he sailed, he dispatched a cable to fifty prominent New Yorkers:

> I am sailing for New York [on the *SS*] *Mauretania* December ninth paying brief visit of inspection instruction scenes my early life's work stop as have not visited America for ten years am unfamiliar with liquor conditions would you kindly consent to serve on committee which would guide me during my few days stay would be deeply appreciated yours respectfully Harry Craddock American Bar Savoy London reply collect.

Craddock sent this cable to New York City's Mayor James J Walker, author Theodore Dreiser then known for his reportage in *The New York Times*, Grover Whalen, Ring Lardner, Irvin S Cobb, OO McIntyre, Marc Connolly, and Karl K Kitchen. It was also rumoured that "one of Craddock's engagements in America will be to shake the cocktails for a party of millionaires aboard a private luxury yacht just outside the 12-mile limit. This he will neither confirm nor deny."

A news article noted that Craddock had to hurry back "because Londoners would never forgive him if his absence deprived them of an essential ingredient of their New Year festivities, a Craddock cocktail."

Just after the repeal bells rang to announce the end of Prohibition in America, a news item announced the proposal of an international bartender exchange with Europe's greatest mixing names shaking it up for thirsty Manhattan imbibers:

> The Ritz [in New York] is to try out an international exchange of bartenders in its pink glowing cocktails rooms, like the swapping of professors at various colleges." Frank Meier of the Paris Ritz, Harry Craddock of the Savoy, and "August" of Berlin's Hotel Adlon were the first three personalities who were proposed.

We never found out if the exchange programme ever came to fruition.

Why did Harry—with his American naturalization papers and passport—not jump at an opportunity to return to New York? Certainly he received offers the moment alcohol became legal. Of course, he did, commenting to one reporter that: "I know that similar offers have been made to fellow-barmen in Paris and on the Riviera. They haven't got so far as terms yet, but I suppose the big hotels would pay something like £10[41] a week."

---

41   Equivalent to $761.65 in today's currency.

The global economy had just been rattled by the Great Depression and Harry was not feeling confident about making a radical shift in his quality of life to return to New York. "Expenses over there would be very high, though," he added, "and I doubt whether any one in a good position would accept such an offer. Anyhow, I am not going. I'm very satisfied here."

THE GUILD

It is one thing to blow your own horn and talk about your own brilliance in a given field. Harry Craddock was not one of those people. He was career barman, a professional hotel barman. "I've been mixing and serving cocktails—and nothing else—all my working life," he once commented.

Like his predecessor Harry Johnson, Craddock felt it was important to the profession to organise bartenders into a guild as the Asociacion del Cantineros de Cuba had done in 1924 in Havana.

Johnson failed during the 1870s to organise bartenders into a trade union entity in New Orleans. But where Johnson failed, Craddock and seven collaborators including William J Tarling, head barman at the Café Royal, succeeded in convincing British bartenders that it was time to make the art of mixing drinks a respected profession. Harry—the "American", the "King of Cocktail Shakers"—was elected as its first president.

In the guild's official publication, "The Bartender", Craddock spelt out the goals of the organisation: to assist in training apprentices, act as an employment exchange, provide the registration of new cocktails as well as standardisation of recipes for popular and classic drinks, to organise competitions for its members, provide free legal advice, and to arrange for a place where bartenders could get together to swap ideas or discuss problems.

During the 1930s, United Kingdom Bartenders Guild had two presidents, William J Tarling and Harry Craddock. The first had published a plethora of recipes that either he created or were part of his venue's repertoire. The second president was not going to let the UKBG live under a single shadow. After Tarling became president, he published the 1937 volume *The Café Royal Cocktail Book*, a compendium of recipes that best demonstrated the broad scope of British bartending knowledge accumulated from UKBG recipe registration submissions.

There are some remarkable surprises on display. More than a dozen tequila drinks such as a precursor to the Margarita plus an equal number of vodka drinks are documented.

Blue Bird
(Invented by WJ Tarling)
½ Vodka.
¼ Cointreau.
¼ Lemon Juice.
3 dashes Maraschino.
3 dashes Blue Extract.
Shake.

Bullfighter
¼ Hercules.
¼ Grand Marnier.
½ Tequila.
Shake.

Central Heater
(Invented by JH Purcell)
¼ Booth's Gin.
¼ Aurum.
¼ Vodka, Wolfschmidt.
¼ Lemon Juice, fresh.
Shake.

Clubland
(Invented by A Mackintosh)
½ Clubland White Port.
½ Vodka (Wolfschmidt).
Dash Angostura Bitters.
Stir.

Devil's Torch
(Invented by H Parker)
½ Vodka.
½ French Vermouth.
3 dashes Grenadine.

Gargoyle
(Invented by G White)
1/3 Vodka.
1/3 Booth's High and Dry Gin.
1/3 Passion Fruit Juice (sweetened).
Put ingredients into shaker half filled with ice, add
one slice of lemon, shake and serve.

Godfrey's Corpse Reviver
(Invented by Godfrey Baldini)
2/3 Gin.
1/3 Vodka.
Dash of Grenadine.
Dash of Angostura Bitters.
Shake.

Govina

(Invented by James Leven)
7/10 Booth's Gin.
2/10 Vodka, Wolfschmidt.
1/10 Orange Juice, fresh.
Dash Pineapple Sirop, Idol.
Mix.

Grand Duchess

Dash of Bitters.
3 dashes Lemon Juice.
2 dashes Grenadine.
2/3 Vodka.
1/3 Jamaica Rum.
Shake.

Green Lady

(Invented by ST Yakimovitch)
1/6 Lemon Juice.
1/6 San Silvestro Liqueur.
2/6 Wolfschmidt Green Vodka.
Shake.

Green Park

(Invented by P Silvani)
1/3 Seager's Gin.
1/3 Latvian Rye Vodka.
1/6 Cointreau.
1/6 Grapefruit Juice, fresh.
Shake.

Grünland

(Invented by Max Miiller)
1 dash Absinthe.
3 dashes Peppermint, green.
1 teaspoonful Lemon Juice.

½ Allasch, Kummell Kor.
½ Vodka.
Shake.

Heddon
(Invented by AJ Duffell)
¼ Vodka, Wolfschmidt.
¼ Lillet.
¼ Blue Curaçao, Bols.
¼ Crème de Noyau, white.
Dash of Lemon Juice.
Shake.

Huntress
(Invented by Charles J Jaeger)
Use Champagne Cocktail Glass,
put in 1 or 2 pieces of Ice, add
1/10 Vodka.
1/10 Orange Juice.
1/10 Cordial Medoc.
7/10 Ice cold sparkling Moselle.
Stir. Decorate with slice of orange.

Jaeger
(Invented by Charles J Jaeger)
1 dash Orange Bitters.
1/7 Grand Marnier.
3/7 Vodka, Wolfschmidt.
3/7 Dry Sherry.
Stir. Serve with cherry and lemon peel.

Jalisco
1/3 Orange Juice.
¼ Teaspoonful Grenadine or
Syrup.
2/3 Tequila.
Shake.

Lenna

(Invented by Heini Schmidt)
2 dashes Grenadine.
½ Vodka.
½ Champagne.
Use Champagne Glass. Stir, serve with a piece of
lemon peel.

Little Tickle

(Invented by F "Fitz" Fitzgerald)
½ Seager's Gin.
¼ Vodka.
¼ Crème Yvette.
Serve with a red cherry. Shake.

Matador

1/3 Orange Curaçao.
1/3 French Vermouth.
1/3 Tequila.
Shake.

Metexa

(Invented by JE Mouncer)
¼ Tequila.
¼ Swedish Punch.
½ Lillet.
Shake.

Mexican Eagle

¼ Jamaica Rum.
¼ French Vermouth.
½ Tequila.
Shake.

Mexico

1/3 Fresh Lime or Lemon Juice.
Teaspoonful Syrup.
2/3 Tequila.
Shake.

Nervo Knox

1/3 Vodka.
1/3 Blue Curaçao.
1/6 Fresh Lemon Juice.
1/6 Fresh Lime Juice.
Shake.

Ole

(Invented by Conrad Rosenow)
1/5 Gin.
1/5 Vodka.
1/10 Cointreau.
½ Champagne.
Stir.

Picador

¼ Fresh. Lime or Lemon Juice.
¼ Cointreau.
½ Tequila.
Shake.

Pinequila

1/3 Pineapple Juice.
2/3 Tequila.
Shake.

Polish Pearl

(Invented by ST Yakimovitch)
1 dash Peach Bitters.
1/3 Danzig Silver Water.

1/6 Baczewski's Antique Liqueur.
1/6 Lemon and Barley Syrup.
1/3 Baczewski's Pearl Vodka.
Shake.

Rio Grande
1/3 Italian Vermouth.
1/3 Gin.
1/3 Tequila.
Shake.

Rose Marie
(Invented by J. "Jimmy" Leven)
7/10 Gin, Booth's.
1/10 Vodka, Wolfschmidt.
1/10 Creme de Noyau.
1/10 Forbidden Fruit.

Royal Toast
(Invented by WE Edwards)
1/3 Vodka.
1/3 Cherry Brandy.
1/3 French Vermouth (Noilly Prat).
Mix.

Sandringham Special
(Invented by J Saunders)
3 dashes Orange Bitters.
½ Canadian Club Whisky.
¼ Grand Marnier.
1/8 Latvian Rye Vodka.
1/8 Apricot Brandy.
Mix. Squeeze lemon rind.

Senorita
1/3 Gin.
1/3 Tequila.
1/3 Fresh Lime or Lemon Juice.
2 dashes Grenadine.
Shake.

Shaitani
(Invented by Alex Scotland)
3/10 Bourbon Whisky (Seagram's).
3/10 Vodka (Wolfschmidt).
1/10 Orange Curaçao (Bols).
1/10 Creme de Noyau.
2/10 Lemon Juice.
Shake.

Sombrero
¼ Italian Vermouth.
¼ French Vermouth.
½ Tequila.
Squeeze Lemon Peel on top. Shake.

Swallow
(Invented by G Siepel)
1/3 Vodka, Latvian Rye.
1/3 Orange Juice.
1/3 Aurum.
Dash Apricot Brandy.
Shake.

Sylvan
(Invented by P Silvani)
1/3 Latvian Rye Vodka.
1/3 Aurum.
1/3 Lemon Juice.
Shake.

Tequardo
(Invented by D. Bennett)
1/3 Tequila.
1/3 Daiquiri Rum.
1/3 Orange Juice.
Shake.

Tequila Cocktail
1/3 Fresh Lime or Lemon Juice.
Teaspoonful of Grenadine.
2/3 Tequila.
Shake.

Tia Juano
1/8 Campari.
3/8 French Vermouth.
½ Tequila.
Shake.

Toreador
½ Tequila.
¼ Apricot Brandy.
¼ Fresh Lime or Lemon Juice.
Shake.

Varsity Blues
(Invented by W Whitfield)
½ Booth's High and Dry Gin.
¼ Vodka (Wolfschmidt).
¼ Bols Blue Curaçao.
1 dash Maraschino (Magazzin).
Mix.

Only 1,000 copies of this record of 1930s British cocktails were printed by the guild, making it one of the rarest and most sought-after cocktail volumes to obtain to this day.

But why are we showing you these drinks? We need to remind you that whilst America was in the doldrums of Prohibition and the Great Depression, British and European bartenders had taken up the mantle, inspired by Craddock's enthusiasm and dedication. They kept the dream alive.

1935: Just like bartenders before him, Craddock endorsed favourite products that he used in his bar.

A very public figure in 1934 and 1935, Harry appeared in an advertisement for Booth's Dry Gin in the *Times of London* and in the UKBG's *The Bartender* (at the time of this writing, we are still searching for a copy of a 1930s Lillet ad we are certain that in which we once saw him appear).

CHAPTER THIRTEEN

FISHING & SUCH

ll work and no play would have made Harry Craddock as very dull person indeed. The cocktail mixer did have a challenging hobby that also got attention in the news: Craddock love fly-fishing.

A humorous story ran in London's *Daily Mirror* about Harry's encounter with Teddy, "the Trout of Trouts", who lived under the at Denham, Buckinghamshire. As the narrator told it:

> At length I put seventeen mayflies on the same line, and phoned up Harry Craddock. ...Harry as you may know, is also one of this world's Famous Fishermen. What Harry doesn't know about trout fishing is just every trout's ambition to find out.
>
> I told him I was trying to catch Teddy, the famous Denham Trout. ...He was most sympathetic. Said he'd take the afternoon off and come down with a cocktail shaker and some special flies he'd collected off the bar counter the night before."
>
> I went back to the bridge and waited. ...Teddy wasn't having any... I'd just got into my first sleep,

when Harry arrived, a miniature cocktail bar under one arm, a box of mixed flies, a net, rod, and gaff under the other.

1936: The complete angler, Craddock never went fishing without his trusty miniature cocktail bar.

"What flies are you using?" he asked.

"Mayflies," said I.

"WHAT???" screamed Harry, before fainting clean away. "Mayflies in July??????!! You might as well try with a CHEESE SANDWICH."

"And that I will," I cried, stung to the very quick.

"In a tizzy I had opened my lunch bag."

You should have seen Teddy the Trout leap upon that sandwich. I jerked the rod and LO, Teddy was mine for the frying. Harry took one piscatorial look, shrieked, and went back into his faint...

Opened on 18 April 1931, on Park Lane, The Dorchester was a five-star property, sporting an American bar—as every fashionable hotel in London had to have to attract A-list clientele. Yet for some reason, management decided to rebuild the ground floor bar, in 1938, and asked Craddock to place a time capsule within its walls as well.

He mixed a Martini, a Manhattan, and a White Lady, sealed them in individual phials, and packaged them in a cocktail shaker along with the recipes and a scroll that commemorated the event. When the bar was once again reconstructed, in 1979, this time capsule was found intact.

A shocking headline appeared on 3 February 1939 "Harry quits the Savoy bar—after 19 years". The accompanying article went on to relate that:

> Harry Craddock, who in his crisp white coat looks like a small-sized bishop, was resting in his flat near Earl's Court[42], wondering what to do. After nineteen years of serving behind the American bar, he has left his job. Another man was in his place yesterday.

The man who took his place was Eddie Clark, who had been tending bar at the Savoy Group's Berkeley Hotel since 1934 and was asked to fill Craddock's shoes until 1942 when he was called to war service. He never returned to the Savoy.

Harry, on the other hand, ended up at The Dorchester's new bar by the time the Second World War was declared on 1 September 1939. Deemed one of London's safest buildings because of its reinforced concrete construction, the hotel itself was the temporary residence of many cabinet minsters including First Earl of Halifax, Edward Frederick Lindley Wood, who replaced Anthony Eden as Foreign Secretary, and the First Viscount Norwich, Alfred Duff Cooper, who was Minister of Information. Winston Churchill had the balcony of his suite walled in for additional privacy during

---

42   Harry lived at 17 Earls Court Gardens, SW5 from at least 1927 until 1940. He moved sometime before the end of the war to 8 Troy Court, W8, putting him at this address in the phone directory in 1944.

his wartime stay. General Dwight D Eisenhower moved from Claridge's to The Dorchester whilst he planned the 1942 D-Day invasion. So cloistered in a veil of military secrecy, Harry shook cocktails for the Allied heroes throughout the Blitz until the war's end.

1947: Craddock as he appeared at age 74, when he retired from The Dorchester.

Maybe it was the stress of the war and rationing. Maybe he was just tired of mixing drinks. Harry Craddock retired in April 1947 from The Dorchester.

But was that really the end of a career that spanned two continents and more landmark watering holes that anyone in the world could wish to have on the resume? No, it wasn't. Situated in the heart of London's ritzy Mayfair district, he was asked to open, in 1951, the refurbished bar at Brown's Hotel. (Even in 1960, a picture of Harry hung in a place of honour at Brown's.)

A couple of days after his 85th birthday, on 31 August 1960, he refuted a few rumours and clarified a couple of things about his life after a reporter commented that: "Friends of Harry Craddock told me he was dead. He died two years ago, they said. ...Yesterday I found him, the who was once the most famous cocktail mixer in the world—celebrating his 85th birthday in an old peoples' home in South Kensington."

It was then we that discover that he mixed drinks for the Duke of Windsor, when he was still the Prince of Wales when the royal summoned him to Buckingham Palace to mix drinks. It was then that he admitted that he mixed cocktails for King George V and King George VI. "In 58 years I worked the bar. I made 25,000,000 cocktails and a lot of money," he noted, "But I gave a lot of it away...you know, odd friends asking for a loan. Now I don't want people to no where I am, living on National Assistance. I feel ashamed."

He wasn't drinking cocktails anymore. "I had so much over 60 years that I don't want any more," the octogenarian admitted. He hadn't had a drink since Christmas that year. The nursing home at 22/24 Ashburn Place in Kensington had given him a great birthday party.

He died there, on 23 January 1963, aged 87 years from a cerebral haemorrhage and vascular degeneration. Caregiver Alice Carroll reported his death. He was buried two days later in a common grave at Gunnersbury Cemetery in Acton.

His step-daughter Louise Emily Fitzgerald had married James Patrick Dillon back in Cork, Ireland, living a quiet life until her own death on 21 January 1993. (Her husband had passed way in 1975 and her son James VC Dillon died in 1984.)

Craddock had not mentored a nephew or other person to take his place like Harry Johnson had done. He lived his life as a hotel bartender and as a hotel bartender he closed the last chapter of his life.

But he provided the world not only with a vibrant story of how the America's Golden Age of the cocktail ended in London, a legacy that was spread onto the European continent and beyond. Harry Craddock gave the world a lasting legacy of why the cocktail lives even today.

CHAPTER FOURTEEN

CRADDOCK'S NEW YORK & LONDON

arry Craddock covered a lot of landmark ground during his career. From the Cotswolds to Manhattan to London, the trail gives you a deep impression of the how and why he became the most celebrated barman at the close of the cocktails' Golden Age. It may not be easy to tour every spot on the globe that he haunts in one go. But this tour will give you an excuse to feel his spirit in both American and Britain.

NEW YORK

Hoffman House, Broadway and 24th Street, New York: Fresh from working in Nassau at the Hotel Colonial, Craddock found a position at the bar manager at this landmark bar until it closed, in July 1915, to make room for a tall commercial structure.

Holland House, Fifth Avenue and 30th Street, New York: It was while he was there, beginning in 1916, that Craddock became a naturalised citizen, something that he expressed his intentions to do when he returned from Nassau five years earlier. He also married Irish widow Annie Fitzgerald and registered for the military draft while he was employed. It's at the Holland House that Craddock allegedly shook the "last cocktail mixed in New York" before he left for London.

Knickerbocker Hotel, Broadway and 42nd Street, New York: Although he rarely mentioned the place in later interviews, Craddock appeared to have worked under James B Regan's direction at this landmark hotel, owned by John Jacob Astor: The breeding ground for other bar greats such as Eddie Woelke.

200 West 80th Street at Amsterdam Avenue, New York: Right after Harry married the widow Annie Fitzgerald, they moved into this Upper West Side. Even when they moved to London, in 1920, they kept the apartment for at least another five years, which Annie's daughter Louise Emily lived in when she moved to New York to find a job and create her own life.

LONDON

American Bar at the Savoy, The Strand, London: Acquiring a position in the dispensary bar on 20 September 1921, Craddock made his name even before he was promoted to head barman of the hotel's American Bar. By the time he left, in 1939, he had change the way the city of London drank with his personality, his media savvy, and his documentation of cocktails as they were at this highpoint in the dawn of the European Golden Age of Cocktails.

The Dorchester, Park Lane, London: Craddock had placed a time capsule containing three drinks in separate phials, accompanied by recipes and a scroll to commemorate the moment while the Dorchester was still rebuilding its bar area in 1938. The hotel offered him a job as its head barman the following year after he quite the Savoy. He stayed there until 1947.

Brown's Hotel, 33 Albermarle Street, London: Another five-star luxury hotel asked Craddock to put his mark on its bar and its cocktail menu, in 1951, when the famed bartender came out of retirement to work on Brown's bar staff and menu for four years. It was from Brown's that he officially called his retirement.

10 Pembridge Crescent, Notting Hill, London: The Craddocks moved into this flat once he secured a job. The family had been living with his older brother Ernest on Devonshire Road in Chiswick.

17 Earls Court Gardens, Kensington, London: Harry lived at this address from at least 1927 until 1940.

8 Troy Court, Kensington, London: Craddock next moved to this address during the Second World War. He stayed there until he moved into the pensioners' home, around 1956, because he had no savings and was dependent upon National Assistance.

22/24 Ashburn Place, Kensington, London: At the age of 87, Harry Craddock passed away at this address, which was a pensioners' home at the time.

Gunnersbury Cemetery, 143 Gunnersbury Avenue, Acton, London: Harry Craddock was buried in a common grave at this cemetery on 25 January 1963. It appears that his step-daughter Louise Emily Fitzgerald Dillon nor any surviving relatives on his side did not care for her step-father's funeral arrangements. But then, he didn't want anyone to see him in his final days.

CHAPTER FIFTEEN

LIQUID SALUTES TO HARRY CRADDOCK

GIUSEPPE GALLO
LONDON, ENGLAND

My favourite Craddock recipe is the Eddie Brown: a delicious combination of London dry gin, bianco vermouth, and apricot brandy. I never have been able to find the real story behind this drink but I always love it because it showcases how vermouth and apricot brandy can bring an extraordinary floral notes to a Gin Cocktail.

Eddie Brown
2 Dashes Apricot Brandy
½ Glass Kina Lillet
2/3 Glass Dry Gin
Shake well and strain into cocktail glass. Squeeze
lemon peel on top.

But my tribute comes from another source. During the last Bar Convent Berlin, we hosted a seminar about the *Arte de Cantinero* book and we created a interpretation of the famous Hanky Panky but with a Cuban touch.

El Cantinero Cocktail

1/3 dark Cuban rum
1/3 Rosolio di Torino
1/3 Fernet Martini & Rossi
Serve in a coupette with a grapefruit twist.

ERIK ELLESTAD

SAN FRANCISCO CA, USA

When combing through *The Savoy Cocktail Book* recipes, I kept coming across Hercules. The general consensus at the time was that Hercules had been an absinthe substitute. The Savoy recipes were so uniformly horrible when made with Absinthe substitutes like Pastis or Ricard, I started doing google.com book searches for Hercules.

Eventually, with the help of friends on eGullet, I came across advertisements for a product called Hercules which would have been available at the time the *Savoy Cocktail Book* was published. However, instead of an absinthe substitute, I discovered Hercules had been an apéritif wine flavoured with yerba maté, of all things. The recipe which follows is one which I have found to work well in Savoy recipes calling for Hercules.

Hercules #5c

1 Stick Cassia Cinnamon, crushed
2 tsp. Coriander Seed, crushed

3 Cardamom Pods, crushed
8 Whole Cloves, crushed
1 tsp Quinine Powder
1 tsp Gentian Root
1 tsp Fennel Seed, crushed
1 tsp dried Peppermint
¼ Cup Yerba Maté
Zest 1 Valencia Orange, 1 Tangerine
½ cup Washed Raw Sugar
(Turbinado or Demerara)
750ml Quady Elektra
(Or other Orange Muscat Wine)
1/4 cup Apple-Ation California Apple Brandy
Combine spices, peels, yerba maté and wine. Heat
to 160 degrees. Filter through fine strainer and add
Brandy. Let stand for at least a day and then enjoy
chilled or where "Hercules" is called for.

ERIK LORINCZ
LONDON, ENGLAND

The Green Park Cocktail, which I proudly serve or offer once the guest has finished the White Lady, is the back bone inspiration for this drink. It's a transformation of a gin-based drink with fresh citrusy notes for a modern palate using fresh basil and celery bitters which create a perfect freshness with delicate taste.

Green Park Cocktail
50 ml Old Tom gin
Fresh basil
3 drops of Celery bitters
30 ml fresh lemon juice
15 ml sugar syrup
Dash of egg white

Blend all ingredients with hand blender on the
bottom of the shaker for 10 second. Add ice shake
hard and double strain into coupette glass. Garnish
with a smile.

I would be sitting at the American Bar at the Savoy, I
would ask Craddock to make me his Corpse Reviver No 2.
Another well balanced drink where each ingredient perfectly
support each other.

H JOSEPH EHRMANN
SAN FRANCISCO CA, USA

My favorite Harry Craddock recipe is the Corpse
Reviver No 2 (and his quote alongside it), because it was
an early inspiration to me in my programme at Elixir and
was one of the classic drinks I often quoted and lead people
two when they were trying to understand what it was that
I was offering at my bar. I would pull out the Savoy and
talk to people about how drinks should be made and the
Corpse Reviver No.2 was one of my particular favourites.

I've been known (like so many) for my Bloody Mary
recipe since the summer of 1992, but I always tried to get
people to understand why other drinks make great "corpse
revivers". I was looking to create something new yet clas-
sically inspired and I came up with the Eldersour. It was a
great success for me both at Elixir and while launching the
Square One brand around the US. It was very much inspired
by my love for the Corpse Reviver No 2.

Eldersour

1.5 oz rosehip-infused Square One Organic Vodka*
1 oz St. Germain Elderflower Liqueur
1 barspoon powdered sugar
1 oz organic egg white (I egg)
Juice of ½ organic lime
Juice of ½ organic lemon
Peychaud's Bitters

Place all ingredients in the mixing glass of a Boston
Shaker, cap and shake for 10 seconds. Remove
tin and fill with ice. Cap again and shaken for 15
seconds. Hawthorne Strain onto a cocktail glass.
Garnish with a few drops of Peychaud's Bitters.

Rose hip-infused Square One:

Remove one drink of Square One from a new bottle
and make yourself a cocktail to drink (certainly
don't throw it away!). Then add 20 dried rosehips
(found in Eastern European, Nordic and other
specialty grocers) per 750 ml of vodka and let sit
for at least 5 days, agitating once daily. Then strain
and discard rosehips, returning infused vodka to its
bottle. Rosehips may also remain in the bottle for
appeal on the back bar, but use a fine strainer to
remove any sediment when serving.

AGO PERRONE
& GABRIELA MONCADA PEÑA
LONDON, ENGLAND

In the Anniversary Cocktail we recall traditional ingredients, a Harry Craddock style sharp cocktail with a hint
of the homemade touch that was one of the many characteristic of Harry Johnson. The final result is an explosion of
flavour with a richness that is carried forward by the nutty
and spicy fragrances.

The Anniversary Cocktail

40 ml aged Jamaican rum
20 ml homemade sherry & hibiscus reduction
20 ml lemon juice
10 ml Galliano Ristretto
2 dashes orange bitters
Shake all the ingredients with ice and serve in a
cocktail glass. Garnish with lemon peel.

Homemade Sherry & Hibiscus Reduction

700 ml Oloroso sherry
25 gr hibiscus flower
5 cardamom pods
Bring to boil and simmer for 30 min; add 250gr
caster sugar.

Our favourite Craddock recipe is the Empire Cocktail.
The ingredients their very own personality, however they
express very well together in a fantastic aromatic experience.
And the name is pretty cool, too.

Empire Cocktail

¼ apricot brandy
¼ calvados
½ gin
Shake well and strain into a cocktail glass.

LUCA CORDIGLIERI

LONDON, ENGLAND

The Chinese Cocktail. I discovered it while researching
for the new cocktail list and I was amazed by the balance of
despite the ingredients sounding sweet. It is now a cocktail I
suggest to my guests. It is also on China Tang's Cocktail List.

Chinese Cocktail
1 Dash Angostura
3 Dashes Maraschino
3 Dashes Curaçao
1/3 Grenadine
2/3 Jamaica Rum
Shake and Strain

The Chinese Cocktail gave me the inspiration for my own recipe and I based it on 1 base spirit, 2 liqueurs, 1 syrup and 1 bitter, which is what makes up the Chinese Cocktail.

1875 Cocktail
50 ml Beefetear 24
10 ml Galliano L'Autentico
15 ml Dry Orange Curacao Pierre Ferrand
5 ml Orgeat Syrup
2 drops Bob's Liquorice Bitter
Shake and strain into a cocktail glass
Garnish with a twist of orange

TAKUO MIYANOHARA
TOKYO, JAPAN

The name of "Corpse Reviver No 2" is a very interesting name and is a the very eye opener cocktail. It is also one of the most famous cocktails of Harry Craddock's and a lot of bartenders have challenged themselves to make their own variation.

The image of this cocktail is of mornings and hangovers, so I have made the most suitable cocktail for an eye opener. My idea for this cocktail is "gas", using an Espuma, which helps to stimulate your stomach. Espuma not only makes gas but also extracts orange flavour from the orange peel I use for this cocktail instead of Cointreau. I also add milk for protecting the tired stomach. The most impressive characteristic of this cocktail is that it is the drink which is injected with CO_2 using Espuma. I can say that this is the real cocktail for a eye opener.

I have named this cocktail "Corpse Reviver Zero" ("Zero" means reset this time.) It's not just for breakfast anymore. But be careful not to drink too much.

Corpse Reviver Zero

40 ml Tanqueray No.10
10 ml Absinthe
20 ml Fresh Lemon Juice
10 ml Canne Sugar
2 tsp Milk
1 Orange peel
Pour all ingredients with crushed ice into an Espuma, and inject CO_2 and shake. Pour into chilled cocktail glass.

MAL SPENCE
GLASGOW, SCOTLAND

I think having spent much of my career tending to hotel bars lends me certain affinity towards Craddock. The fact he never received a penny for his seminal bar book also makes me pang with relative sympathy. Although McElhone is a fellow Scotsman, and created some of the most popular classics, it is with Craddock I side with in the White Lady debate, Craddock's version being a much more palpable concoction.

Despite this, it is probably with resounding fraternal similarity, that I cite Craddock's Corpse Reviver No 2 as my favourite of his.

The marrying of the botanical notes of the gin with absinthe serves as an eye opening drink no matter which time of the day it is consumed. The sharpness of fresh lemon juice, held back with the sweetness of Cointreau, rounds out a bracing, well balanced drink. This timeless classic, serves as influence to my own revitalizing cocktail in tribute to Harry.

Keeping the formula of equal parts the absinthe and Cointreau are replaced with yellow chartreuse, keeping the herbal notes and sweetness intact but creating an altogether differing drink.

Embassie
1 part Dry Gin
1 part Cocchi Americano
1 part Fresh lemon juice
1 part yellow Chartreuse
Shaken, strained, straight up, lemon twist.

RUSTY CERVEN
LONDON, ENGLAND

My favourite drink? Can't be anything else than Corpse Reviver No 2.

But there is one drink what I made about year ago and would love to share with you. It is a twist on the Bentley Cocktail from the *Savoy Cocktail Book*. The original recipe calls for one part of calvados and one part of Dubonnet. So I kept these two ingredients, modified the balance, enhanced it with more aromas from umeshu (sweet plum wine), and cut it down with Peychaud's Bitters.

When I tried it first time, I was blown away with the result. The name for me was really catchy since there is a Bentley shop just cross the square. There was no doubt in my mind to keep it are the name of my drink as well.

Bentley No 2
2 dashes Peychaud's Bitters
30 ml Dubonnet
30 ml Akashi Tai Umeshu (sweet plum wine)
45 ml Calvados
Stir all ingredients in mixing glass, strain into cocktail coupe over one chunk of ice and garnish with grapefruit zest.

ADAM EDDY BURSIK
BRATISLAVA, SLOVAKIA

I have a cocktail that is inspired by Harry Craddock and Harry Johnson together. A combination of whiskey, Pernod, gomme syrup, fresh lemon juice, and homemade saffron bitters. It's called the "130th Flower".

In 2013, exactly one hundred thirty flowers will decorate the graves of these two amazing, visionary bartenders—one flower for each year of their passing.

This particular flower is served in liquid form, I hope for many years in honour of these unique personalities. The 130th Flower combines flavours that remind me of Harry Craddock as Pernod, Harry Johnson as whiskey, and little bit of my own personality as saffron.

130th Flower

5 cl Chivas Regal 12 years Old
1 cl Fresh Lemon Juice
1.25 cl Gomme Syrup
2 dash Saffron Bitter (homemade)
6 drops Pernod
Stir well and strain into an old-fashioned glass on
a big piece (floe or berg) of ice. Squeeze lemon peel
on top.

SUSIE WONG

MANCHESTER, ENGLAND

My favourite competition drink? It could well be my
entry for the 2011 "Rock The Farm" cocktail competition.
Here I used Craddock's White Lady Cocktail as my inspiration. I employed the original recipe as my "canvas" being:
Gin, citrus and liqueur. To modernise it I added beetroot
and for balance used a good quality blackcurrant liqueur
with apple lending itself as a little lengthener.

All these ingredients married together create an "earthy"
yet refreshing take on the great classic!

Root To Gin

37.5ml Chase Elegant Gin
12.5ml Chase Blackcurrant Liqueur
2-3 drops of Bitter Truth celery bitters
50ml Apple Juice
15ml Lime Juice
6 grams Beetroot
Muddle chopped up beetroot. Add all ingredients.
Shake and fine strain into a coupette. Serve with
beetroot crisps.

BLAIR FRODELIUS
SYRACUSE NY, USA

Since Harry Craddock worked in the Savoy, I decided to use English and European ingredients. Of course, Regan's bitters weren't around when Harry was behind the stick, but gaz regan (aka: Gary Regan) is an ex-patriot, like Harry. Bringing it all back around.

As for the name of this cocktail, I'm sure that Harry spent many a hour chatting over drinks with fellow bar and pub lover, Gilbert Rumbold. It is in great part due to Rumbold's bold and amusing Art Deco illustrations in the *Savoy Cocktail Book*, that it was an outstanding success and has continued to stay in print for over 80 years. I think Harry would have created something along these lines for him.

Rumbold
1.5 oz Plymouth gin
0.75 oz Pimm's
0.75 oz Dubonnet Rouge
3 dashes Regan's Orange Bitters
Stir with cracked ice and strain into chilled cocktail
glass. Garnish with orange twist.

PETE JEARY
LONDON, ENGLAND

Based on the classic Gimlet as featured in the *Savoy Cocktail Book*, and proving very popular on the Hawksmoor menu!

Sweet, Velvety Gin

60 ml Plymouth Gin
10 ml Homemade Rhubarb Syrup
20 ml Egg White
Triple shake*, single strain. Serve in a port/sherry
glass.
*Dry shake, then with ice, then dry shake once
more.

Based on the 'Froth Blower Cocktail' from the *Savoy Cocktail Book*.

Navy Strength Gimlet

50 ml Plymouth Navy Strength
15 ml Homemade Lime Cordial**
Stir and strain into a chilled Martini glass.
**Add grated zest of five large limes to 500 gr caster sugar and 500 ml boiling water. Let steep for 5 minutes and stir in 1 tbsp (15 ml) citric acid powder. Strain and cool. Makes approx 750 ml cordial.

My favourite drink though is probably the Corpse Reviver No 2. It's the perfect balance of strength and flavour, is ideal for drinking at any time of day, and is simple enough that it can be recreated anywhere. It's also helped me through a LOT of very foggy mornings!

ESTHER MEDINA
LONDON, ENGLAND

One evening I started drinking Negronis followed by Gibsons. Then I thought about the fathers of our craft and I had the idea to deconstruct are reassemble the drinks. The bartender thought I was mad but he was presently surprised when he tried my concoction. The drink was christened by a couple of good friends a wee while after.

Gin est belle
50 ml Plymouth Gin
25 ml Noilly Ambre
(or a combination of Italian
and French style vermouths)
Stir, up, lemon twist discarded. Served with pearl
onions soaked in Campari on the side.

I couldn't possibly choose between a White Lady and a Corpse Revival No 2, both of them are genius drinks that I enjoy very much.

SIMON ROWE
LONDON, ENGLAND

My favourite Savoy drink has to be Millionaire No 1, a true classic and a big favourite in The Bar at The Dorchester: a real harmony of flavours.

Soi sage (Be wise)
45 ml Plymouth Gin
25 ml Bergamote Liqueur Crema
20 ml Lemon juice
15 ml Sage syrup
10 ml Plymouth Sloe Gin
Shake and strain first four ingredients and float
on top of the sloe gin in a sage and sugar rimmed
crusta glass. Garnish with a sage leaf and spoon (to
combine the floated drink)

LEE POTTER CAVANAGH
LONDON, ENGLAND

One of my favourites because I believe it sticks out now as not fitting with the rest of the Savoy drinks is the Ping-Pong Special. When you read through this as well as his use of blue vegetable extract in the Blue Monday and Blue Train Cocktails, you see what I mean.

These stick out as names or styles of drinks that gained favour for all the wrong reasons in recent history. Do me a favour next time you go into the Savoy dressed in your finest, channel Mr. Craddock and ask for a blue drink straight faced. If they complain or try to take the mickey out of you, point out these two drinks. Sorry Jacob Briars, you were only about 70 years behind Harry! Anyway, here's my attempt to restore this drink to something befitting the pantheon of Savoy and Craddock cocktails, a time when drinking blue drinks was smooth, sophisticated and indulgent, not tongue in cheek.

The Gossamer Years
1/3 Plymouth Navy Strength Gin
1/3 Plymouth Sloe Gin
1/3 Cocchi Barolo Chinato
(or another red china/kina/quina)
1 dash Bob's liquorice bitters
(Angostura will do in a pinch)
1 bar spoon quality Earl Grey tea,
for smoking the glass
1 lemon twist, for garnish
Grab a cocktail coupe and fill it with iced water.
Place the Earl Grey tea onto a plate and using a
crème brulee sized blow torch, burn the tea. When it
begins to form an ember or glow, empty the coupe

into the sink and upend over the tea to catch the
smoke. You need the water in the glass beforehand
to better catch the smoke and the ice will make sure
the glass is still cold when you get the drink.
Pour all other ingredients into a mixing glass, add
cubed ice and stir for roughly 20-25 seconds to ensure sufficient chilling and dilution. Using a strainer
pour the drink into the now thoroughly smoked
coupe. Garnish with a lemon twist ensuring that
your express all the oils over the surface.

NATHAN MERRIMAN
LONDON, ENGLAND

I had the privilege and honour of re-opening the American Bar at the Savoy. I remember the first time I made this
cocktail at 1:30 PM in the afternoon for a guest who had
travelled from Japan to experience his dream of visiting
the American Bar: His choice of drink being Savoy Hotel
Special Cocktail No 2. A simple, yet effective drink. I must
admit I have had the pleasure of drinking this a couple of
times since.

I really enjoy the touches the quinine from the Dubonnet lingers has: a soft background with the herbs and spices
blending with the French vermouth. Plymouth Gin harmo-
niously brings all these ingredients together with its creamy
full body, fresh aromas of citrus, coriander and juniper. It
has a long, fresh lingering finish which both the Dubonnet
and French vermouth support beautifully.

My favourite recipe from the *Savoy Cocktail Book*:

Savoy Hotel Special Cocktail (No 2)

2 dashes Dubonnet
1/3 French Vermouth
2/3 Plymouth Gin
Shake well and strain into a cocktail glass. Garnish
with orange peel on top.

Both Harry Johnson and Harry Craddock are considered trailblazers to me. They created a legacy, a path for others to follow and be guided by with recipes to inspire, learn, and teach. They are pioneers of the cocktail craft and movement and will be for decades, if not centuries to come.

The Trailblaze Cocktail

50 ml Plymouth Navy Strength Gin
7.5 ml Carlshamns Flaggpunsch Swedish Punsch
Liqueur
2.5 ml Aalborg Taffel Akvavit
2.5 ml Cane Sugar
2 dashes Bokers Bitters
Stir and strain into pre-chilled Club at The Ivy
Coupette. Garnish with a lemon twist. Discard.
Drop a small block ice in cocktail to keep chilled.

PHIL DUFFY
LONDON, ENGLAND

One of the many things I like about the *Savoy Cocktail Book* is the occasional appearance of slightly wacky or extinct ingredients, frequently written in the book with no explanation or background. Swedish Punch, Kina Lillet and Pimento Dram represent the familiar end of this spectrum, but are also joined by the likes of Caperitif, Hercules, and Charbreux.

My homage to this is in the use of Ramazzotti, which is not the rarest of products but all the same not often found behind London's bars. This is mixed with a healthy dose of Chartreuse—a liqueur greatly favoured throughout the book—and a couple of dashes of orange bitters. A 50 ml measure of Plymouth is added and the whole is stirred down and put in a nice cocktail glass. Garnished with a lemon twist, which gets my vote for second greatest garnish of all time (beaten only by the banana dolphin, which is admittedly a little less versatile).

Another wonderful feature is the intermittent notes to drinks; for example to the Alaska Cocktail: "...it was probably thought of in South Carolina, hence its name". In honour of the slightly irreverent tone of Mr Craddock, the above drink is called the Clapham Cocktail, because I invented it in Mile End.

My favourite Plymouth drink in the *Savoy Cocktail Book* has to be the Hoffman House cocktail, followed closely by the Turf Cocktail. The Hoffman House gets it because it is quite simply the best Martini recipe I know: 2 parts Plymouth, 1 part French vermouth, 2 dashes orange bitters and a lemon twist on the top. Beautiful simplicity and balance, with no hint of a quest for the driest Martini. Even a banana dolphin couldn't improve it.

Clapham Cocktail
50 ml Plymouth Original
20 ml Ramazzotti
15 ml green Chartreuse
2 dashes orange bitters
Shake well and strain into a cocktail glass, garnish
with a lemon twist.

ANDREAS CORTES
LONDON, ENGLAND

With this cocktail I wanted to go back in time to that golden age of bartending. Back then, flavours were a lot bigger, bolder and more brash, when you drank the drink it was the base spirits and flavours on show and the importance of balance, rather than a focus on technicality and showmanship.

I have used Plymouth Sloe Gin, a true British winter tradition; korenwyne, the flavouring agent for genever and the inspiration for English gin; cognac for body and heat; and finally to support the korenwyne, rosé champagne. This adds a dryness to the cocktail and a slight astringency in order to achieve the sought-after balance. We are also very interested now at looking at champagne as a wonderful ingredient and addition to a drink, rather than something to add a bit of fizz. I also find that the flavours of Plymouth Sloe Gin, korenwyne, and rosé champagne really complement each other.

The Craddock Reviver
35 ml Plymouth Sloe Gin
15 ml Bols Korenwyne
7.5 ml VSOP Cognac
15 ml Laurent Perrier Rosé Champagne
All ingredients stirred together in a mixing glass and
strained into a chilled Martini glass. Garnish with
an orange twist and a cherry.

Harry Craddock created possibly one of the most important works for bartending in the 20th century. Although after reading a lot of his recipes and various blogs out there, it would seem that a lot of his drinks were updates or twists on older cocktails created by the very first bartenders in some of the oldest bars in America. Although I am not saying that he did not create some fantastic drinks on his own, I would like to focus on this point. After all here is a man who has come from the fast paced, centre of cocktails historically, New York, to dreary old cognac and gin drinking London.

He had this great opportunity to drag London kicking and screaming into the modern and sophisticated world of choice and 'classy' drinks, which he did marvellously, and in no small way has contributed to London now being the epicentre of cocktail culture in the world. You would most certainly be right in saying that without the savoy cocktail book a lot of old recipes, methods and ideas from the early days of bartending would have been lost forever.

On this note I would like to talk about the Aviation cocktail. Although originally accredited to Hugo Ensslin of the Hotel Wallick in New York, Craddock stripped it of créme de violette, upped the sour component, and made it far more palatable to the English.

For me it is a cocktail with three components that ticks all the boxes. It is fresh, lively and balanced and the main star, Plymouth Gin, is supported and enhanced, not covered up. You may also assume that this cocktail could have been the inspiration behind possibly his most famous White Lady Cocktail but I suppose only Mr Craddock would know If that was true or not.

LESZEK STACHURA
COPENHAGEN, DENMARK

I love the White Lady Cocktail. It's just an absolutely amazing drink so I decided to make a tribute to Harry making a twist on White Lady. I wanted to keep it very simple were the balance is just absolutely crucial and make the whole composition dancing together like a prime ballet. I wanted to make an old school drink simple but very complex with the biggest emphasis on the base ingredients and to combine classic and region, so I decided to use Bols Barrel-Aged Genever as the closest as we can get to old school flavour back from the days combined with one of the most influential ingredients used in the kitchen in Scandinavia (where I have lived for past seven years) which is liquorice.

The idea was to combine the sweet, salty, earthy, spicy bitterness from liquorice with the genever. For me, the genever characterizes those lovely malty, bready notes with hints of citrus and some peppery notes that comes from rye; a bit of earthy and a little spice from the barrel aging in Limousin oak. Beautiful.

I added, of course, some lemon juice to balance the sweetness and improve the citrus plus a small hint of orange liqueur Cointreau to complement. (I was thinking of the dry Pierre Ferrand curaçao. But it would have made the drink too flat. The liquorice is too strong, too pronounced a flavour. It would make the drink too flat, too one-dimensional. That extra sweetness from Cointreau makes it just perfect—multidimensional.) The result over-exceeded my expectations.

First when you put the drink close to your mouth you get a tingling, teasing fragrant note of lemon zest) with a little note of liquorice, then you take a sip and the magic starts. You get that amazing fresh, malty taste of the genever with a hint of sweetness from liquorice that turns into fresh citrusy delight that slightly turns it way to lick of saltiness and rounds up at the end through the peppery spiciness to that unique bitterness of liquorice and again sweetness balances it out and that hint of spice. It just keeps dancing together with a cashmere texture in the mouth feel.

The Golden Lady
6 parts (60 ml) Bols Barrel Aged Genever
or Bols Genever
1 part (10 ml) Cointreau
2.2 parts (22.5 ml) Fresh lemon juice
(freshly squeezed off course)
1 part (10 ml) rich liquorice sugar syrup*
Shake hard for 7 seconds. Fine strain into a chilled
cocktail glass. Garnish with lemon zest sprayed and
discarded.
*2kg sugar, 1kg water, 30 gr of liquorice powder

PETER DORELLI
LONDON, ENGLAND

The first absinthe available in the UK after it had been outlawed elsewhere was from Prague. Hill was the name. I wondered how I could use it. And I knew that absinthe was a favourite ingredient of Harry's so I decided to use it in the White Lady, made long with lemonade.

Harry on the Hill
½ London dry gin
¼ Cointreau

1/8 absinthe
1/8 lemon juice
Egg white
Shake. Top up with sparkling lemonade. Garnish
with slice of lemon.

ALEX KRATENA
& MONICA BERG

LONDON, ENGLAND & OSLO, NORWAY

We love both Craddock and Johnson, however our true favorite is Chrysanthemum Cocktail from the *Savoy Cocktail Book*. We enjoy it because it has a wonderful taste profile, as well as it is very different from many other libations as there is no spirit base. Reading the recipe you almost feel it won't work, however the result is simply delicious and truly amazing! That's why we have created a double twist and named in our mother tongues. True to the original, one for her and one for him, symbolizing our relationship, styles and personalities, salute!

Krysantemum (For him) by Monica Berg

60 ml Bache Gabrielsen Pineau des Charentes
30 ml DOM Bénédictine
7.5 ml Ardbeg 10-Year
5 ml Apple cider Vinegar
50 ml Pilsner Urquell
Stir all ingredients in mixing glass apart from beer,
strain into chilled coupe. Garnish with a spray of
lemon zest and discard. Serve beer on the side in a
stemmed shot glass.

Chryzantema (For her) by Alex Kratena
60 ml Aperitivo Americano Cocchi
25 ml DOM Benedictine
5 ml Suze
50 ml Ruinart Blanc de Blanc
Salvador Dali Dalissime
Freeze dried lychee, rose water, fresh raspberry
Stir all ingredients in mixing glass apart from champagne, perfume, lychee, rose water and raspberry, strain into chilled coupe and top up with champagne. Wrap the stem of the glass in luxury golden tissue and perfume with Salvador Dali Dalissime perfume, lemon zest (discard), dehydrated lychee soaked in rose water inserted with raspberry.

ALESSANDRO PALAZZI
LONDON, ENGLAND

The cocktail that I like from Harry Craddock is The White Lady. It's probably a common choice but it brings back memories of when I first learnt to make cocktails at my catering school but it is also a timeless classic that serves as the inspiration for the base of many cocktails that I recreate because the simplicity of The White Lady proves that using good ingredients allows you to make many fine cocktails. Even to this day, it is a cocktail that I suggest often to customers who aren't cocktail savvy and it gives me an opportunity to speak about Harry Craddock.

The DUKES "Time" Martini
60 ml Frozen Plymouth Gin
infused with lemon thyme*
3 Drops of DUKES dry vermouth
5 ml of "100 Erbe" Liquor (Italian)

Top up with about 15ml of frozen Plymouth gin
and finish with a twist of organic Amalfi lemon and
serve in a frozen martini glass.
* The method of the infused Plymouth gin is as
follows: Place 4 sprigs of fresh lemon thyme in the
bottle of Plymouth gin and add a long zest of organic Amalfi lemon and leave the bottle in a warm place
for 4 days and then freeze it.

GARETH EVANS
LONDON, ENGLAND

I had bought cocktail books before I bought *The Savoy
Cocktial Book*, but they all had one thing in common—they
were list of recipes. The *Savoy* to me was more a snapshot
of a particular time in history, with short, snappy, spirit led
drinks being the order of the day. It reads to me like a badly
transcribed notebook, with its odd mix of apparently inter-
changeable measurements, odd use of grammar and Unnec-
essary Capitalisation, and I love the strange little descriptors
for cocktails (Snowball cocktail—"this is woman's work"),
but to be honest, this only serves to endear it to me further
—it's almost like talking to the great man himself. Gilbert
Rumbold's illustrations with their faintly inappropriate and
outdated captions help to give the book a sense of history as
well ("Picture of Portly Butler of Proud Lineage, expressing
utter consternation upon inadvertently opening the door to
quite a few Gay Young Things" is a highlight), and one only
has to look at the recent *PDT* cocktail book's similar style
to see how influential this book has been.

To me though the most important thing I got from this
book is actually in the introduction, and it is something I
teach to my bartenders to this day. Harry's tips in the "A Few

Hints For The Young Mixer" are all sound and true, but the one that sticks with me is his instructions on how to shake a cocktail: "Shake the shaker as hard as you can: don't just rock it: you are trying to wake it up, not send it to sleep!"

This is my favourite drink in the book, and a drink I make at least once a week for a guest. It is to me the perfect way to show what I think a cocktail should be; simple, elegant, balanced, and approachable. I always use this as a drink to show people that say they hate gin that the stuff they got smashed on in their parent's liquor cabinet shouldn't define their adult drinking habits. It nearly always persuades them to give that most famous of English spirits another try. Although the recipe doesn't mention a garnish, I think the drink benefits from a twist of lemon over the drink.

Fine & Dandy Cocktail
¼ Cointreau
¼ lemon juice
½ Plymouth gin
1 dash Angostura bitters
Shake and strain.

My drink is a twist on possibly Harry Craddock's most famous creation—The White Lady, using the best of British to work with the Plymouth. I swapped out the Cointreau for Chase rhubarb liqueur, which works brilliantly with gin, reduced the lemon juice and added another souring element in its place: yoghurt acid powder. This is my favourite ingredient to use at the moment, it adds a beautiful creamy sourness to the drink, without altering the texture The White Lady is so revered for, and heightens the brightness from the gin.

I hope Harry would approve, and perhaps even honour me with a highly inappropriate caption of my own.

Modern British Lady

50 ml Plymouth gin
20 ml Chase rhubarb liqueur
10 ml lemon juice
Egg white
1 barspoon yoghurt acid
Dry shake, add ice and hard shake. Fine strain into a chilled cocktail glass, and garnish with 3 cubes of poached rhubarb vacuum infused with Plymouth.

ACKNOWLEDGEMENTS

An intense labour of love such as this mission to pay tribute to remarkable men such as Harry Johnson and Harry Craddock has taken a few years to achieve. Along the road a number of people have lent their hearts and hands throughout the research and writing. For this we raise a White Lady Cocktail to Peter Dorelli, Erik Lorincz, and Mauro Majoub for opening up their files and contributing a few photos and insights.

Paying such loving tributes in liquid form to this work, we have to thank in alphabetical order a fabulous group of bartenders from around the world:

Adam Eddy Bursik, The Rum Club, Bratislava, Slovakia
Ago Perrone, The Connaught, London, England
Alessandro Palazzi, Duke's at Duke's Hotel, London England
Alex Kratena, Artesian Bar at the Langham Hotel, London, England
Andrea Montague, Callooh Callay, London, England
Andreas Cortes, Claridge's, London, England
Blair Frodelius, Good Spirits, Syracuse NY, USA
Erik Ellestad, Heaven's Dog, San Francisco CA, USA

Erik Lorincz, The American Bar at the Savoy, London, England

Esther Medina, Opium, London, England

Gabriela Moncada Peña, Beaufort Bar at the Savoy, London, England

Gareth Evans, Social Pollen Street,London, England

gaz regan, Bar Rags LLC, New York NY, USA

Giuseppe Gallo, Martini & Rossi, London, England

H Joseph Ehrmann, Elixir, San Francisco CA, USA

Jamie Boudreau, Canon Seattle, Seattle WA, USA

Jason Kosmas, The 86 Company, Dallas TX, USA

Lee Potter Cavanagh, HIX Soho, London, England

Leszek Stachura, Studiestræde 5, Copenhagen, Denmark

Luca Cordiglieri, China Tang at The Dorchester, London, England

Mal Spence, Kelvingrove Café, Glasgow, Scotland

Mauro Majoub, Mauro's Negroni Club, Munich, Germany

Monica Berg, Aqua Vitae, Oslo, Norway

Nathan Merriman, The Club at The Ivy, London, England

Peter Dorelli, formerly head barman of the American Bar at the Savoy, London, England

Pete Jeary, Hawksmoor & Pete's Ginger Brew, London, England

Phil Duffy, Pernod-Ricard UK, London, England

Rusty Cerven, , The Connaught, London, England

Simon Rowe, The Dorchester, London, England

Simone Caporale, Artesian Bar at the Langham Hotel, London, England

Sumire Miyanohara, Bar Orchard Ginza, Tokyo, Japan

Susie Wong, Bar Epernay, Manchester, England

Takumi Watanabe, The Sailing Bar, Nara, Japan
Takuo Miyanohara, Bar Orchard Ginza, Tokyo, Japan

Then there are the wonderful financial contributors who donated to our indiegogo.com campaign to fund the acquisition of some of the illustrative materials for this project as well the printing of 500 limited edition, signed and numbered, hardcover copies. Those people include Blair Frodelius, Bruce Tomlinson, Gelbes Haus, Jamie Boudreau, Nick Wineriter, Adam Peters-Ennis, Paul Mathew, Domenico Maura, Nick Detrich, David T Smith, Emma Stokes, Adrian Vipond, Rolf Neill, Karen Nielsen, Christopher Carlsson, Paul Bradley, Chris Hoy, Timothy Ward, Dean Callan, Lukasz Stafin, Paul Lambert, Michael Menegos, Divyesh Chauhan, Yves Cosentino, Kevin Cockerell, Andy Seach, Nick Bell, Dimi Lezinska, Mike Tomasic, Dennis Tamse, Timo Siitonen, Rohan Jelkie, Daniel Oliver Warren, Kimmo Aho, Dimitris Kiakos, Stefan Schifter, Amy Jenkins, Mark Holt, and Alan Cartolano.

We raise our last glass to some special people who supported our efforts in very special ways over the past few years as we unveiled portions of our research in master classes, a couple of very special walking tours, and presentations at trade events. Hats off to Sue Leckie, Shawn Kelly, Simon Ford, Giuseppe Gallo, Max Warner, Rachel Hutton, Bastian Heuser, Helmut Adam. We couldn't have continued searching and refining our findings without you!

INDEX

NOTE: Entries set in **bold** are cocktail recipes.

CPSIA information can be obtained at www.ICGtesting.com
Printed in the USA
LVOW071409190413

329963LV00006B/852/P